Faith, Diversity, and Education

This volume explores how conservative Christian schools are shaping education in America and, in turn, students' attitudes about diversity.

Based on data collected as part of a year-long, ethnographic study of a K–12 conservative Christian school in the South, this volume analyzes the way that diversity was thought about and acted upon in a school and how these decisions affected students and teachers across racial differences. The book demonstrates that conservative Christian theology defined a school's diversity efforts. It also reveals the complexity of addressing diversity in a context that is largely wary of it, at least in its typical secular usage. The findings presented in the book raise important questions about school vouchers, the influence of religious beliefs on educators' decision making in schools, the morality and existence of Christian schools, and diversity initiatives in white spaces.

Faith, Diversity, and Education: An Ethnography of a Conservative Christian School will be of great interest to researchers, academics, and postgraduate students in the fields of education, sociology, and religion.

Allison H. Blosser is Assistant Professor of Education at High Point University, USA.

Routledge Research in Religion and Education

Series Editor
Michael D. Waggoner
University of Northern Iowa, USA

Comparative Theology in the Millennial Classroom
Hybrid Identities, Negotiated Boundaries
Edited by Mara Brecht and Reid B. Locklin

God, Education, and Modern Metaphysics
The Logic of Know "Thyself"
Nigel Tubbs

Migration, Religion, and Schooling in Liberal Democratic States
Bruce A. Collet

Teaching Religion Using Technology in Higher Education
Edited by John Hilton III

Public Theology, Religious Diversity, and Interreligious Learning
Edited by Manfred L. Pirner, Johannes Lähnemann, Werner Haussmann, and Susanne Schwarz

Religious Education as a Dialogue with Difference
Fostering Democratic Citizenship through the Study of Religions in Schools
Kevin O'Grady

Investigating Political Tolerance at Conservative Protestant Colleges and Universities
George Yancey, Laurel Shaler and Jerald H. Walz

Faith, Diversity, and Education
An Ethnography of a Conservative Christian School
Allison H. Blosser

For a full list of titles in this series, please visit www.routledge.com

Faith, Diversity, and Education

An Ethnography of a Conservative Christian School

Allison H. Blosser

NEW YORK AND LONDON

First published 2019
by Routledge
52 Vanderbilt Avenue, New York, NY 10017

and by Routledge
2 Park Square, Milton Park, Abingdon, Oxon, OX14 4RN

Routledge is an imprint of the Taylor & Francis Group, an informa business

© 2019 Taylor & Francis

The right of Allison H. Blosser to be identified as author of this work has been asserted by her in accordance with sections 77 and 78 of the Copyright, Designs and Patents Act 1988.

All rights reserved. No part of this book may be reprinted or reproduced or utilised in any form or by any electronic, mechanical, or other means, now known or hereafter invented, including photocopying and recording, or in any information storage or retrieval system, without permission in writing from the publishers.

Trademark notice: Product or corporate names may be trademarks or registered trademarks, and are used only for identification and explanation without intent to infringe.

Library of Congress Cataloguing-in-Publication Data
A catalog record for this book has been requested

ISBN: 978-1-138-54941-8 (hbk)
ISBN: 978-1-351-00059-8 (ebk)

Typeset in Sabon
by Apex CoVantage, LLC

For Joe, the most faithful justice seeker I know

Contents

Acknowledgments		viii
Series Editor Foreword		xi
1	Why Care About Christian Schools?	1
2	Grace Academy: Unapologetically Christian	25
3	Prioritizing Fit: Grace Academy's Recruitment and Retention Practices	45
4	Cultivating a Climate of Diversity and Unity	68
5	A Hidden Curriculum of Diversity	90
6	Lessons From Grace Academy	118
	Final Thoughts	136
	Appendix: Methodology	140
	Index	152

Acknowledgments

This book—one largely about faith—is incidentally the result of lot of prayer, both my own and those of many others. I first conducted this study as a part of my dissertation, with the singular purpose in mind of completing my PhD program. I wondered for some time whether or not it would have life beyond the dissertation. But the words of one of my committee members, Dr. Williams, kept ringing in my ears. He had pulled me aside at my graduation and told me that he thought it would make a great book. Still, I hesitated to rework it and publish it as one. Then Donald Trump got elected president and appointed Betsy DeVos as Secretary of Education, and education and the experiences of minority groups in this country were forever changed. I knew that Grace Academy's story could speak to the policy changes the Trump/DeVos administration were proposing. So here we are.

Lots of people made this book possible. One of those people is Dr. D, the head of school at one of the Christian schools where I used to teach. After I went to him lamenting and wanting to address my students' obvious prejudicial attitudes toward others, he put me on the school's first diversity committee. It was then when I first began thinking about Christian understandings of diversity and what that meant for Christian schools. From there, my study was born.

I also want to thank all the professors who've taught me along the way. I am especially appreciative of my academic mentors, Kate Phillippo and Patty Kubow, who advised me professionally throughout this project. Kate, in particular, believed in this project from day one when it was just an idea for a dissertation, but she too then encouraged me to turn it into a book. I am also thankful for the feedback of my other dissertation committee members, Rhys Williams and Leanne Kallemeyn, who offered me guidance throughout the study.

My family has been an amazing support network as well, and this book wouldn't have been possible without them. My parents and stepparents all demonstrated what it is to choose careers and ventures that have real impact. My mom, in particular, always modeled that, and more than once, she convinced me I was supposed to write this book. My in-laws too are servant leaders and have been some of my biggest cheerleaders. They watched my kids so I could write and often reminded me to "breathe" when I was stressed. I also want to specifically acknowledge my sister-in-law, Tracey, who was the first nonacademic to read a draft of this manuscript. She too helped convince me to publish it as a book because she said that people like her (a mom of kids in private school) would want to read it.

I am indebted as well to my fabulous colleagues and Department Chair, Dustin Johnson, as well as Dean Tillery, Provost Carroll, and President Qubein at High Point University, who encouraged me, believed in the importance of this work, and supported my course release award in the fall of 2018, which allowed me to finish the book. I also owe a big debt of gratitude to the librarians at HPU, who went out of their way to locate the resources I requested.

And I want to thank my editors, Mike Waggoner and Matt Friberg, who were immediately interested in the manuscript and who have been available to me every step of the way. Also, thanks to the Routledge reviewers who gave me incredibly helpful feedback when the book was still in the proposal stages.

I am grateful too for my friends (too many to name here) and the people in my church community, who've cheered me on, prayed for me, and told me all along I could do this, even when I doubted myself. I am especially thankful for my dear friend, Natasha, who urged me to write the truth in this book, even if it ends up being hard to hear, because truth can bring about justice and change.

I want to recognize all of the wonderful faculty, staff, parents, and students of Grace Academy, who welcomed me into their school, prayed for me, trusted me, and confided in me. I know it wasn't easy to make themselves and their school vulnerable. I am especially thankful to Dr. Smith, who devoted countless hours of his time answering my questions and telling me his vision for GA. His passion for addressing diversity was palpable, and he felt from the beginning that our work together was divinely inspired. He was willing and eager to learn from my study, and I hope this book's final chapter demonstrates that he did. He never lost site of the bigger picture—the potential for other schools to learn from GA's efforts and missteps—and hopefully, they will.

I want to thank my kids, Seth and Bea, for being constant reminders that how we do school and what we teach our youth matters, and for making me periodically close my laptop to answer their questions, hug them, or read them a story. I love you two so much.

Most importantly, I could not have finished this book without the support of my husband, Joe, a true partner in every sense of the word, which is why this book is dedicated to him. Joe, you've been there for me throughout the entire process of crafting this book. You let me debrief with you after long days of observing and interviewing. You've read countless drafts of this manuscript from its inception as a dissertation to its final form years later as a book. You've watched the kids and even took them for a week so I could write. You've encouraged me along the way and convinced me that this book matters. You've helped me keep my eyes set on justice. You've made my book your priority, and I cannot thank you enough.

Series Editor Foreword

The opening years of the 21st century brought increased attention to religion as an important dimension of culture and politics. Early in this period, the dramatic multi-pronged attacks of September 11, 2001, came as a jolting reminder of the potential for violent action that can have bases in religious motivations. Over the same period, we came to see an increase in religiously motivated activity in politics. In the US, we see this as an evolution from the Moral Majority movement led by televangelist Jerry Falwell that emerged as a force in the late 1970s as the beginning of the New Religious Right. On further reflection, however, we can see the involvement of religion extending much further back as a fundamental part of our social organization rather than a new or emerging phenomenon. We need only recall the religious wars of early modern Europe through to the contentious development of US church and state relations as evidence of the long-standing role religion has played as a source of competing values and beliefs. That said, there has been a significant upturn in research and scholarship across many disciplines relative to the study of religion in the last decade and more. This is particularly the case in the area of the relationship of education and religion.

While religious education—study *toward formation* in a particular faith tradition—has been with us for millennia, study *about* religion as an academic subject apart from theology is more recent. Whereas theology departments proceeded from religious assumptions aiming to promulgate a faith tradition, the religious studies field emerged as a discipline that sought to bring a more objective social scientific approach to the study of religion. The origins of this approach date back to the European research centers that influenced US scholars beginning in the 18th century. The formalization of this trend, however, is a fairly recent phenomenon, as illustrated by the 1949 formation of Society for the Scientific Study of Religion with its own scholarly journal and the creation of religious studies departments across the US in the wake of the US Supreme Court decision in 1963 that allowed teaching *about* religion (rather than *for*) in public education institutions. It was also that same year that the American Academy of Religion was born out of a group of scholars that had since 1909 been meeting under the various names related to biblical study.

It is out of this relatively recent increase in scholarly attention to religion and education that this book series arises. Routledge Publishers have long been an important presence in the respective fields of religion and of education. It seemed like a natural step to introduce a book series focused particularly on Research in Religion and Education. My appreciation extends to Max Novick for guiding this series into being and now to Matthew Friberg, for continuing Routledge's oversight.

In this book, the 13th volume in the series, Professor Allison Blosser gives us a rich ethnographic study of a conservative Christian school's attempt to address diversity. It is the first such book-length ethnography of this particular kind of context in more than 30 years—a period during which enrollment in these kinds of schools has increased by 40% (Blosser, 2017). This study is instructive on more than one level. First, regarding its methodology; it illustrates the care that it takes for a researcher to gain entry, to establish trust, and to negotiate relationships in an environment that can be suspicious of "outsiders'" motivations to study their environment; there have been unfortunate examples of attempts at exposés that rightfully make these places cautious of such requests for access.

Second, Blosser gives us a deep and, it seems to me, true picture of the school's genuine attempts to reconcile conservative Christian theological positions with secular societal pressures for diversity, some tenets of which they perceive to be at odds with their values. For example, we see the differences that become apparent due to the internal diversity within Christianity regarding biblical interpretation—a study in the power dynamics of who decides what is most important to draw from the Bible and how that is decided. For example, why do they include race, ethnicity, socioeconomic status, and differing ability in their definition, but not religious difference or sexual orientation?

It is also apparent the critical difference that leadership can make. One highly motivated leader in a position of significant influence on hiring and curriculum development can make some things happen. By the same token, we realize that such a leader must have an exceptional combination of knowledge and skills to deal with the different constituents of the school, including donors, school boards, teachers, parents, feeder churches, and prospective families. Professor Blosser deftly brings to light the challenges leadership faces in assumptions and attitudes that exist within and across these groups, and what is required to address concerns while moving the diversity initiative forward.

Conservative Christian schools have long been a part of the PK-12 landscape in US education and are expected to continue to increase. Although they represent a small percentage of the US school population, their cultural impact remains significant, as a they are an influential preparatory environment for future citizens in our democracy, many of whom go on to conservative Christian higher education and work in organizations that share these cultural beliefs. Their experiences with and attitudes toward diversity that they carry into our shared civic life will be forged in schools like the one in this study. This book gives us important contemporary insight into the processes that give rise to conservative Christian ideas about forming dispositions toward diversity in their schools.

Michael D. Waggoner
Series Editor
Research in Religion and Education

1 Why Care About Christian Schools?

Lighthouse Christian Academy in Indiana made national news in May 2017 when US Representative Katherine Clark questioned Secretary of Education Betsy DeVos about the school's discriminatory practices. Clark pointed out how the school accepts $665,000 in public dollars via school vouchers, yet it also reserves the right to deny admission to families in which homosexuality is practiced or alternative gender identities are acknowledged. Clark wanted to know if such practices would be permitted under President Trump's proposed federal voucher program. Tri-City Christian School in New Hampshire also made the news for telling a transgender student he was no longer welcome at the school (Associated Press, 2017). And conservative Christian universities are equally present in the media. Liberty University, for example, made headlines when its president, Rev. Jerry Falwell Jr., overwhelmingly supported Donald Trump in the 2016 presidential election despite Trump's inflammatory comments against minorities, immigrants, Muslims, and women. These incidents reinforce the public perception that US conservative Christian schools and the evangelicals who support them do not welcome diversity. But is that true? Or is the issue of diversity in Christian schools[1] more complex?

Approximately 700,000 US students attend conservative Christian schools (NCES, 2017).[2] While that number may seem inconsequential, it becomes significant when one considers that Christian schools 1) have a history of practicing discrimination, 2) are primed to grow, and 3) are increasingly being funded by public dollars. If such schools are indeed teaching or practicing discrimination, the wider public has a right to be concerned. Just what Christian schools teach, however, has largely been a mystery to those who do not attend them because access to them can be hard to obtain. Once inside a conservative Christian school, though, the reality is more complex than news reports reveal. Many Christian schools are striving to teach students about diversity and prepare them for life in a pluralistic society, but what this means differs from what non-conservative Christian scholars and the wider public would expect.

2 Why Care About Christian Schools?

A Discriminating Past

When it comes to diversity, many conservative Christian schools are reputed to promote controversial positions, such as the belief that homosexuality is sinful (Peshkin, 1986), that women are subservient to men (Peshkin, 1986; Rose, 1988, 1993; Stitzlein, 2008), and that Jews are inferior to Christians (Schweber & Irwin, 2003). And, historically, Christian schools are remembered for their practice of racial discrimination in admissions (Blosser, 2017; Chou et al., 1982; Flowers, 2005; Gutmann, 1987; Nevin & Bills, 1976; Parsons, 1987; Rose, 1988, 1993). After the 1954 *Brown vs. the Board of Education* decision that required the integration of public schools, many Christian schools opened with the explicit purpose of giving parents the option for their kids to attend "whites only" schools. These schools, which came to be known as "segregation academies," were especially prevalent in the South, where there was greater resistance to integration than in the North (Blosser, 2017; Chou et al., 1982; Flowers, 2005; Nevin & Bills, 1976; Parsons, 1987). It wasn't until 1970 that the IRS began to crack down on Christian schools practicing such racial discrimination. That was the year the IRS claimed such schools would no longer be tax-exempt, and around 100 schools lost their exemptions (Blosser, 2017; Chou et al., 1982; Rose 1993). Thirteen years later, in 1983, issues of tax-exempt status related to racial discrimination surfaced again, but this time, the issue made its way to the Supreme Court. The IRS had declared that Bob Jones University could no longer claim its exemption because the school forbade interracial dating (Blosser, 2017; Parsons, 1987). The Supreme Court sided with the IRS in an overwhelming margin of eight to one (Blosser, 2017; Parsons, 1987), claiming that the government has a "fundamental, overriding interest in eradicating racial discrimination in education" (*Bob Jones v. United States*, 1983).

In the present day, some researchers claim that Christian schools do not foster in students the skills and values needed to participate in a democratic society, like the valuing of diverse points of view (Blosser, 2017; Godwin, Ausbrooks, & Martinez, 2001; Rose, 1993; Sikkink, 2009) or the ability to thoughtfully weigh different life choices (Blosser, 2017; Gutmann, 1987, 1999; Rose, 1993; Sikkink, 2009; Wagner, 1990). Some scholars, however, offer evidence suggesting that such claims are unfounded (e.g., Green, 2006; Godwin et al., 2001; Godwin, Godwin, & Martinez-Ebers, 2004; Sikkink, 2009).[3] Given Christian schools' historical practice of racial discrimination and scholarly disagreement over their present practices, then, our national conversation about school choice and the public funding of Christian schools via vouchers needs an in-depth study of how Christian schools think and act on issues of diversity. This book is the product of such a study. It is designed to help people understand what is going on in these schools and the kinds of students they produce. It will ultimately help us have a more informed public conversation.

A Growth Trend

Christian school advocates will often point out that the first schools in the US were Christian schools (Wagner, 1990). Advocates make this claim because the purpose of schooling in colonial America was to help students "delude" Satan by teaching them Christian values, how to read the Bible, and to memorize scripture (Rury, 2016). The earliest textbooks, like the New England Primer, contained distinctly Christian content. Even the post-Revolution "common schools" of the 19th century, the precursor to today's public schools, were decidedly Protestant in nature, so there was little need for separate, privately run Christian schools until the 20th century (Rury, 2016). That said, a few Protestant Christian groups, such as German Lutherans and the Missouri Synod, established their own schools in the mid-19th century (Russo, Soules, Newman, & Douglas, 2018). But the schools that can today be classified as conservative Christian didn't become popular until the 1960s, after a series of Supreme Court cases in the early 20th century began outlawing religious practices, such as scripture readings and prayer, from public schools (Russo et al., 2018). The Christian School Movement was largely seen as a reaction to the decline of shared Protestant values in public schools, peaking in the 1960s and 1970s when as many as two new Christian schools were opening every day (Wagner, 1990).

The 1960s and 1970s were also part of the period in the history of American evangelicalism known as the Fourth Great Awakening (Rose, 1988). The Fourth Great Awakening was characterized by "chronic uneasiness and cultural disorientation" (Rose, 1988, p. 25) largely brought on by widespread protests and changes in the social fabric of America that threatened the "supremacy and legitimacy of the traditional, white Protestant, middle-class, patriarchal family" (Rose, 1988, p. 33). As Rose (1988) described, "The evangelical response of the Fourth Great Awakening was to call again for a return to the values of 'old time religion that had made America great'" (pp. 25–26). It is, of course, no coincidence that President Trump capitalized on this sentiment in his campaign slogan and was overwhelmingly supported by white evangelicals (Burton, 2018).

Christian schools today are purposefully separatist. They believe that Americans can no longer turn to a shared set of Protestant values that dominate our social institutions. From their perspective, public schools no longer serve the explicit purpose of acculturating people into a culturally Protestant American way of life (Parsons, 1987),[4] which is an issue for conservative Christians who wish to unite the institutions of family, school, and church (Rose, 1988). Christian schools are growing (Blosser, 2017; Green, 2006; Zehr, 2005), and their percentage of total private school enrollment is increasing (CAPE, 2017). Christian schools are growing for many reasons. One reason for their growth is that their advocates have an ideological opposition to public education. As Parsons (1987) writes, "Conservative Christians view society as sick and view the public schools as agents of sickness" (p. 6). In fact, 52% of conservative Protestants, as compared to only 29% of mainline Protestants, feel that public schools are "hostile to their moral and spiritual values" (Sikkink, 2009, p. 282).[5] Specifically, conservative Christians accuse America's public schools of promoting "secular humanism," a religion they claim to be devoid of moral values (Blumenfeld, 2012; Flowers, 2005, p. 117; Rose, 1988, p. 1, 1993, p. 456).[6] As Sikkink (1999) explains, "Conservative Protestant opposition to a 'secular' public schools system is thought to drive the increasing supply of and demand for non-public schooling, such as Christian schools and home schooling" (p. 52).

Modern social and cultural conditions likewise push families away from public schools and toward alternatives. Sikkink (1999) claims that many characteristics of modernity, like industrialization and a rationalized education system defined by formal and secularized standards, encourage feelings of alienation from public schools. Other characteristics of modernity are "increasing geographic mobility and cultural pluralism" (Sikkink, 1999, p. 54), which make it more difficult for Americans to have a dominant set of shared values, particularly Protestant values, that public schools can teach (Parsons, 1987; Peshkin, 1986; Sikkink, 1999). In addition, "the loss of social ties within the extended family, workplace, religious organization, and neighborhood that bind parents of children in a particular school makes it difficult for a school to gain legitimacy from its ties to the community" (Sikkink, 1999, p. 55). So families turn to Christian schools because they don't feel loyal to their public school, whereas in Christian schools, there are shared and identifiable Christian values.

Changes in the religious landscape are also promoting the expansion of Christian schools. In the same way that conservative Christians are dissatisfied with the secular nature of public schools, Americans are increasingly rejecting the secularization of mainline Protestant churches in favor of more conservative sects (Finke & Stark, 2005; Yeakley, 2011). In addition, of the 70% of Americans who identify as Christian, around a quarter of them identify as evangelical Christian (Pew Research Center, 2015). Christian schools are part of the highly nested, dense network of organizations that make up the growing landscape of conservative Protestantism, which is "characterized by distinctive organizational templates, behavioral norms, and symbols of shared purpose that facilitate the proliferation and coordination of organizational activity" (Stevens, 2002, p. 349). Thus, Christian schools have numerous organizational resources at their disposal that are provided by sponsoring churches and denominations, Christian publishing houses, and Christian school associations (ACSI, 2014; CSI, 2014; Parsons, 1987; Peshkin, 1986; Rose, 1988, 1993; Stevens, 2002; Wagner, 1990).

Further, as Christian schools grow, they are likely to become more diverse. For starters, the US student population overall is becoming more diverse in many ways (e.g., ethnically, racially, socioeconomically, religiously). And evangelicals themselves are increasingly more racially diverse as well. Only 64% of American evangelicals identify as white, and half of evangelicals under the age of 30 are nonwhite (Public Religion Research Institute, 2016 as cited in Bacon Jr. & Thomson-DeVeaux, 2018). Some of the growth in Christian schools will likely come from the Latino population since an increasing number of Latinos living in the US are becoming evangelical Christians (Bacon Jr. & Thomson-DeVeaux, 2018; Miller, 2012; Pew Forum, 2007). Most significantly, the growing popularity of voucher programs will increase the diversity of Christian schools as more—primarily low-income—students are able to afford to attend these schools.

Accepting Public Funds

Everyone pays for Christian schools. Public tax dollars in the form of school vouchers are being used to fund Christian schools across the nation. There are currently 25 voucher programs in the US (Education Commission, 2017), and this number will likely expand over the next decade with the support of several powerful political entities, like the current Secretary of Education, Betsy DeVos, who is a staunch advocate of school vouchers and attended, financially backed, and sent her children to Christian schools. DeVos also claimed that her education agenda is one that will, in her view, "advance God's Kingdom" (Green, 2017). Her foundation has donated millions of dollars to private Christian schools, charter schools, and other organizations seeking to privatize education and/or organizations opposed to the separation of church and state (Rizga, 2017). Moreover, in 2018, President Trump and Secretary DeVos proposed a budget that included over a billion dollars to support school voucher programs and other choice initiatives while cutting billions of dollars from programs that support public schools (Strauss, Douglas-Gabriel, & Balingit, 2018). Similarly, in 2017, House of Representatives Bill 610, also known as *The Choices in Education Act*, aimed to introduce federally funded school vouchers. And at the state level, powerful legislative organizations, such as the American Legislative Exchange Council, are fighting for more school choice programs, and states are beginning to lift legal regulations that have been preventing them from adopting voucher programs (Strauss, 2017).

In many school voucher programs, religious schools are the primary recipients of voucher dollars (Anti-Defamation League, 2012). In North Carolina, 93% of voucher students attend religious schools, while only

6 *Why Care About Christian Schools?*

70% of all students attending private schools in North Carolina attend religious schools (Helms, 2016). Christian schools are particularly attractive to voucher recipients because they tend to have lower tuition costs than other types of private schools (CAPE, 2014). As evidence of this trend, in North Carolina, eight of the top-ten requested schools by voucher recipients were Christian schools (Helms, 2016).

The obvious question arising from voucher programs is whether vouchers violate the US Constitution's Establishment Clause—that is, the separation of church and state—given that public funds are supporting sectarian schools that promote a specific religion. The 2002 *Zelman v. Simmons-Harris* Supreme Court case has presumably settled that issue, though opponents of vouchers, like the Anti-Defamation League (2012), disagree with the Court's reasoning. In the Zelman ruling, the Court maintained that the government, via the voucher program under question, was not showing any favoritism toward sectarian schools (*Zelman v. Simmons-Harris*, 2002). Rather, the program was "was one of 'true private choice,'" wherein "families were eligible to receive vouchers and schools to participate, 'without reference to' whether or not they were religious" (Berg, 2003, p. 154). Further, the Court noted that individuals were being awarded the funds, not the schools themselves, and that it was the choice of families, not the government, as to which school would receive their funds (*Zelman v. Simmons-Harris*, 2002).

Another recent Supreme Court case (*Trinity Lutheran Church of Columbia, Inc. V. Comer*), however, approved public funds to be paid directly to Christian schools. In the 2017 decision, the majority opinion suggested that the state grant funds intended to purchase recycled tires to improve playground safety were part of a "neutral and secular aid program," and refusing the payments to sectarian schools would violate the Free Exercise Clause (American Bar Association, 2017, p. i). While the decision was narrowly written, the concurring opinions gave hope to many private school advocates that the Court might be open to programs that provide more public dollars directly to Christian schools.

The spread of vouchers and the public financing of Christian schools is bound to force the question of whether such public financing entitles the wider public to know what is being taught in them. Mawdsley and Russo (2013) suggest it might. As they mention, there is a statutory provision in Ohio that states that schools cannot "teach hatred of any person or group on the basis of . . . religion" (p. 369), which could be a slippery slope for voucher-accepting schools. The authors (2013) ask if, for example, a school could be accused of teaching hatred if "in the course of classroom instruction or liturgical preaching, teachers or clergy refer to the errant beliefs of other religion faiths" (p. 369). A similar argument recently surfaced in a North Carolina courtroom. The primary reason the courts found North Carolina's voucher program unconstitutional was that the state did not hold private schools accountable for what they taught (Dunlap, 2014; Prangley, 2014; Strauss, 2013). Judge Hobgood declared, "Appropriating taxpayer funds to unaccountable schools does not accomplish a public purpose" (Dunlap, 2014).[7] He went on to say that private schools "have no legal obligation to teach them (students) anything" (Dunlap, 2014). Judge Hobgood's and the North Carolina Constitution's use of the term "public purpose" is particularly noteworthy because it encourages the public to ask the question, should the content that private schools teach be accountable to the public?

In response to that question, a study conducted by the League of Women Voters examined the curricula of 75% of the top voucher-receiving schools in North Carolina between 2014 and 2018 (Bechard, 2018). They found that 76.7% use a biblical curricula and argued that the curricula "does not prepare these students for 21st century colleges or careers" (Bechard, 2018, p. 3). The report that emerged from the study explained how the University of California is an example of a major university system that does not accept such a curriculum as fulfilling the minimal entrance requirements in multiple subjects (namely, science, literature, government, and history). The League finds that problematic given that vouchers are funded by taxpayers. Consequently, the League makes the following recommendations:

> We urge the Governor or the University of North Carolina, which administers the Opportunity Scholarship Program, to appoint a commission to review the curriculum used in these literal biblical worldview schools and determine if this curriculum satisfies academic rigor requirements by North Carolina colleges and universities, as well as other major universities outside North Carolina. This commission should also consider if there are clear goals and expectations for what students are learning and should learn in order to prepare for careers in the 21st century. Finally, the commission should make recommendations for curriculum requirements for schools receiving tax-payer funding through Opportunity Scholarships.
> (Bechard, 2018, p. 4)

The report concludes that any school receiving public money should have to use a state-approved curriculum (Bechard, 2018). The question for Christian schools then, of course, becomes how to make themselves distinctively Christian if their curriculum isn't biblical or in line with their theology.

Another question that emerges with the public funding of Christian schools is if schools funded with public dollars are responsible for nurturing democratic citizens. Some scholars question whether Christian schools are producing students who are capable of respecting the viewpoints of people different from them, a skill considered necessary for participation in a democratic society (Blosser, 2017; Godwin et al., 2001,

2004; Gutmann, 1987; Sikkink, 2009). Levinson and Levinson (2003) write,

> It is generally agreed that citizenship in a liberal democracy requires that one tolerate and even respect people who are different from oneself, who hold different beliefs and engage in actions and life practices that are unfamiliar, discomfiting, or even repugnant.
>
> (p. 103)

Gutmann (1987) makes a similar assertion.[8] She (1987) also maintains that while Christian schools may argue that the "welfare of democracy does not depend on all schools teaching common democratic values," the schools do in fact "shar[e] citizenship in [our] religiously and racially diverse society" (pp. 119–120). Arguably then, Christian schools, especially if they accept public dollars, may very well be responsible for such democratic instruction.

Yet some scholars describe Christian schools that do, in fact, encourage students to explore many perspectives (e.g., Green, 2006) and facilitate interethnic friendships (e.g., Candal & Glenn, 2012; Godwin et al., 2001). One study (i.e., Godwin et al., 2001) based on questionnaire data collected from students in Christian schools, non-Christian private schools, and public schools even found that private schools do a better job of fostering democratic citizenship.[9]

Another key part of the public discussion in light of the growth of Christian schools—and the influx of public money—is whether they will be allowed to discriminate in keeping with their religious beliefs (Anti-Defamation League, 2012; Jones, 2013; Mawdsley & Russo, 2013; Wagner, 2014). Voucher opponents argue that because vouchers are state funded, states' constitutional articles on discrimination apply. For example, voucher opponents in North Carolina claim that many Christian schools' admissions policies violate the state's constitution, which states, "No person shall be subjected to discrimination by the state because of race, color, religion, or national origin" and that "the power of taxation shall be exercised in a just and equitable manner, for public purposes only" (Wagner, 2014).

And so, as part of the national voucher debate, Christian schools are being publicly scrutinized for their discriminatory policies, specifically those that deny enrollment and employment to lesbian, gay, bisexual, transgender, and questioning (LGBTQ) students and staff. For example, public opposition to Myrtle Grove Christian School's admissions policy concerning LGBTQ students influenced its decision not to accept the North Carolina state voucher (Blosser, 2017; Jones, 2013; Wagner, 2013). Jones (2013) reports that there are several hundred more schools in North Carolina alone with policies similar to Myrtle Groves' and that Georgia's voucher program has been under attack for the same reason.

Why Care About Christian Schools? 9

Americans United for the Separation of Church and State maintains that it's unconstitutional for public funds to go to sectarian schools and that "publically funded discrimination is a systemic problem" (Jones, 2013). Though many states do not have laws making discrimination against LGBTQ individuals illegal (Bendery, 2014), Christian schools that accept vouchers are increasingly facing public pressures that may force some of them to change their policies.

It is not, however, only discrimination against LGBTQ students and parents that is drawing attention to Christian schools. There are a variety of private schools whose policies allow them to refuse applicants with learning disabilities or those who are English-language learners (Wagner, 2014). And then there are Christian schools who deny admission based on religious affiliation, rejecting Mormons, Buddhists, Jews, Muslims, Unitarians, Jehovah's Witnesses, and more (Wagner, 2014). For example, Grace Academy, the school described in this book, did not have a formal policy to deny admission based on religion, but it had several requirements that could potentially deter non-Christian students from applying. For example, the school required a pastor's recommendation and an essay about the student's relationship with Christ. Parents also had to sign a form consenting to a Christ-centered education (GA's Application for Admission, 2013). The school could theoretically deny applicants who did not fulfill these requirements or did so in an unsatisfactory manner, though I have no evidence that they did so.

With such conflicting evidence, it is problematic that no one has recently gone into a Christian school to conduct an in-depth, qualitative study to inform this discussion. Christian schools remain largely under-researched. This is because it's exceptionally hard to gain access to the schools—stakeholders are skeptical of how "secular" scholars perceive them. Federal research dollars also tend to favor research agendas concerning public schools.

This book, though, fills that void. It informs the debate over the constitutionality of school vouchers and other kinds of public funding. In this story of a Christian school, it demonstrates that neither the school's admissions practices nor the majority of its diversity teaching are in line with the secular consensus of what constitutes public interest. This, however, would not be a surprise to those at Grace Academy, because they didn't want to produce secularly minded citizens. Their faculty and staff mostly rejected secular culture in their teaching, *and* yet they saw public voucher dollars as a means to increase the diversity of the student body, which was a stated goal of the school. They wanted to be more diverse, but they wanted to do diversity on their own terms. Essentially, there was a tension between the school's need to accommodate secular culture enough to receive vouchers and the simultaneous need to reject it in keeping with their religious views. The findings discussed in this book, then, should prompt researchers, policy makers, private school stakeholders, and the wider public to consider developing accountability measures for voucher-accepting private schools and the possible implications if they do.

The Story of Grace Academy

With all the confusion around Christian schools and their growing impact on the educational landscape, I wanted to learn what happens in them. Specifically, I sought to understand what they were thinking and doing about diversity. I gained such an understanding through an ethnographic study of one Christian school. This book presents what I found there and sets the findings within the wider context of education scholarship and public policy debates in the US.

The book tells the story of Grace Academy (GA),[10] a predominantly white, K–12 Christian school in the South. I chose to conduct my research at GA for many reasons,[11] but the most important reason was that it had an explicit and public commitment to address diversity, making the school an "information-rich" case to study (Patton, 2002, p. 230). I spent a full year getting to know GA, observing all facets of school life, including classes, lunch, field trips, service projects, chapel services, faculty meetings, parent meetings, and more. I also conducted formal interviews with 60 members of the school community, including students, teachers, administrators, staff, parents, and board members, and I collected many school documents, such as marketing materials, class assignments, admissions applications, and job postings.[12]

In order to understand how GA addressed diversity, I turned to organizational theory. Organizational theory is particularly conducive to the study of religious organizations because "religious activity is institutionalized and carried out through formal organizations," like schools (DiMaggio, 1998, p. 7). Specifically, I analyzed the school's organizational sensemaking about diversity. Sensemaking is largely about meaning-making. That is, it occurs in organizations as people process and frame information in a way that dictates behaviors and decisions (Blosser, 2017; Evans, 2007). I utilized sensemaking theory as my framework knowing that diversity could mean different things in different contexts and that organizations could address it in various ways (Blosser, 2017). Further, organizational sensemaking also occurs when the status quo is interrupted and people must figure out how to respond to the interruption (Weick, 1995). For GA, the interruptions were the arrival of a new, more progressive head of school and an almost simultaneous recommendation from the school's accrediting organization to address diversity in the school. Consistent with the theory, I did not specifically define diversity from the outset of the study because I understood that the school could have a different understanding of diversity from my own. Instead, I held open that diversity could refer to a broad array of background characteristics (Katz, 1999). School stakeholders' words and actions provided evidence for organizational sensemaking about diversity (Evans, 2007; Weick, 1995).

Sensemaking theory is particularly suited to the study of organizations that function as open systems because they have to make sense of outside information (Weick, 1995). Despite Christian schools' reputation for being separatist, "total" institutions (Peshkin, 1986), Christian schools are open systems. They are exposed to many of the same educational messages as public schools and often feel pressure to respond to the messages in an effort to compete with public schools. Wagner (1997) explains how "research undertaken in Christian schools found a good deal of accommodation to the surrounding American popular culture and the culture of educational establishment" (p. 20). She (1997) elaborates: "They [Christian schools] pattern themselves after one another, and after public schools" (p. 20). Moreover, Christian schools are held accountable by accrediting bodies and tuition-paying parents, and they interact with the colleges and universities that accept their students. The rapid growth of Christian schools also indicates that they rely on resources from their theological environments (e.g., churches, para-church organizations, denominations). Beckford (1973) goes so far to claim that it is impossible for any religious organization to be isolated from the environment. Thus, because Christian schools are in continual interaction with their educational environments (e.g., other private schools, public schools, colleges and universities, accrediting bodies) and theological environments, and diversity is a fairly ubiquitous issue among educational and religious organizations, it was important that I treat Christian schools as open systems and consider how entities in the schools' environments were influencing sensemaking about diversity.

Sensemaking in organizations is also "grounded in identity construction," meaning that sensemaking is largely shaped by stakeholders' need to protect the identity of the organization with which they are affiliated (Weick, 1995, p. 18). Organizations protect their identity through carefully selecting issues to which to respond (Weick, 1995). Private schools, in particular, have several reasons to be concerned with their organizational identities. Foremost, it is the school's identity in which parents are investing. Private high schools, in particular, also recognize that a school's identity affects the way colleges and universities view its students. Moreover, private schools that are affiliated with particular churches or denominations, as are many Christian schools, have an added challenge in that they function as "hybrid-identity organizations"—that is, they have multiple authorities (e.g., churches, denominations, school boards) to which they must answer and therefore multiple identities that they must craft, promote, and maintain (Whetten, 2006, p. 226). How a school makes sense of diversity and its changing demographics is no doubt tied to the school's identity maintenance and formation.

Organizational sensemaking is largely shaped by the organizational context, which can include "embedded values, beliefs, and assumptions" (Evans, 2007, p. 161) and especially the organization's governing ideology (Weick, 1995). DiMaggio (1998) claims that religious organizations tend to have powerful cultures with clearly communicated values that shape and pervade its activities. Such values can shape organizational sensemaking, as they serve as a lens through which members filter new information (Evans, 2007; Pratt, 2000; Weick, 1995). Religious ideology certainly shaped the way GA's stakeholders made sense of diversity.

Organizational context is broader than values and ideology, though. It can also include its administrative structure. Spillane et al. (2002) explain that structure can shape sensemaking since people often have different and sometimes competing interests, depending on their position in an organization. They (2002) note how this is particularly true in schools because principals have different objectives and answer to different people than do teachers. Similarly, organizational structure often dictates relationships within an organization as individuals are often grouped into divisions and/or form informal relationships. Coburn (2001) accordingly found that teachers' sensemaking was shaped by their informal associations with other teachers. And other contextual elements in schools have also been shown to shape sensemaking about diversity, such as the school's racial composition (Evans, 2007), as well as the school's curriculum, the school's mission and history, and the school's policies (Brown, 2011). All of these elements featured prominently in sensemaking about diversity at Grace.

In addition to being shaped by organizational context, sensemaking in organizations is shaped by individuals' worldviews, prior experiences, professional roles (Coburn, 2004; Spillane, Reiser, & Reimer, 2002), and background characteristics, such as their racial identities (Evans, 2007). Coburn (2004) observed that teachers' worldviews mediate environmental messages and that messages that are highly congruent with teacher worldviews are more likely to make their way into classrooms. Phillippo, Brown, and Blosser (2018) found in a study of a teacher preparation program that teacher candidates' sensemaking about relational practices was influenced by the candidates' prior professional experiences with students. Perception of professional role has also been shown to shape educators' sensemaking about policies and practices. This was the case with educators' practice of peer assistance and review in a school district in California (Goldstein, 2004). And Evans (2007) found that principals' racial identities largely shaped their sensemaking about changes in their schools' racial compositions. At GA, sensemaking was similarly influenced by school stakeholders' worldviews, prior experiences with diversity, professional roles, and background characteristics.

My Social Position and Accessing the School

Just as worldviews and prior experiences shaped school stakeholders' sensemaking about diversity, so too did my own social position shape my data collection and analysis. Prior to conducting this study, I had no relationship with GA. I selected GA as a potential research site because it met the sampling criteria I determined at the beginning of the study.[13] After identifying GA as a potential site, I scheduled a meeting with the head of school, Dr. Smith. I learned quickly that Dr. Smith was open and even eager to let me conduct the study because he was the person responsible for creating GA's first diversity initiative. But he also explained that he alone couldn't make the decision to grant me access because diversity was a particularly sensitive issue at GA. According to Dr. Smith, this sensitivity was due to the administration having just let go of the school's first black teacher for poor performance, and racial tensions among members of the school community were high. He was concerned that my study might ruffle some feathers and that I might make the school look bad. He told me I'd first need the support of his administrative team and then the school's accrediting organization, the Association of Christian Schools International. ACSI's support was essential, he explained, because school stakeholders trusted that ACSI would have the school's best interest at heart. ACSI wouldn't approve any researcher whose intent was to denigrate the school. Further, ACSI was largely concerned with the spiritual development of the school, so he believed that having its endorsement would help school stakeholders see that my project could help further the spiritual mission of GA and, potentially that of other Christian schools. And ACSI had already told GA in its recent review of the school that it needed to address diversity, so Dr. Smith thought the organization would support my study.

My background also played a role in my ability to negotiate access. I was, to use Schweber's (2007) terminology, an "insider-outsider" (p. 62). I was an insider in that I am Christian, though I do not currently identify as evangelical, and I had previously taught at two conservative Christian schools. I am also white, heterosexual, and married to an ordained minister of a mainline Protestant denomination. We are members of a mainline Protestant church, though it's a church whose name might suggest it's more conservative than it is. I was upfront about where I attended church, my prior teaching experience, and my husband's religious affiliation/ordination in my early meetings with school leaders. All of that said, I didn't realize until after I had begun collecting data at the school just how much my background as a teacher at conservative Christian schools helped me gain access to Grace. I say this because I learned that most Christian schools require their faculty to ascribe to the school's doctrinal commitments. I imagine the school administrators assumed that because

I taught in similar schools, I must believe in the doctrinal commitments similar to their own, such as the infallibility of the Bible. Those were perfectly fair assumptions, and I had, in fact, signed confessions of faith when I taught at those schools. At the time I accepted those positions, though, I didn't give much thought to what I was signing. I knew I was a Christian and accepted the statements on the contracts as underlying tenets of all Christianity, not really understanding the implications of those beliefs. In other words, at that point in my life, I didn't really know what I believed or didn't believe about the Bible and, frankly, finding out wasn't all that important to me. I was mainly concerned with figuring out how to teach. It was actually only when I began systemically studying the implications of various beliefs on students and teachers at GA that I really thought about the meaning of the doctrinal commitments I had signed and realized that if I were asked to sign such a document today, I could not do so in good faith. In fact, much to my surprise, conducting research at Grace was *both* a spiritual and academic pursuit for me, as I began to pay attention to the theological differences among Christians and learned a lot about what I do and do not believe. The longer I was at Grace, the more I began feeling less like an insider-outsider and more like an outsider based on my own religious understandings. These feelings were challenging because I began developing close (though still professional) relationships with school stakeholders. But, ultimately, I learned through my research at Grace that my Christian faith informs my desire to seek justice for the marginalized and oppressed.

After my first meeting with Dr. Smith, I contacted a staff member of ACSI, an African American man recommended to me by Dr. Smith. After a lengthy phone conversation with him about my study's design, goals, and contemporary relevance, the staff member agreed to write me a letter of support for my project. After the school received ACSI's letter of support, I scheduled a meeting with the school's administrative team and public relations coordinator. Some of the administrators I met with were a bit reluctant to let me conduct the study, but after convincing them that I wasn't there to write an expose of the school, they gave their consent. They did, however, ask if they could offer feedback on my interview questions because they were not convinced that I would get honest or meaningful responses if I asked questions about diversity from a secular perspective, which had been my original approach. They made me aware that my initial research questions were not written in a way that allowed me to understand a conservative Christian approach to diversity. One principal told me I would get secular answers with secular questions. Thus, I immediately learned that GA stakeholders defined themselves in opposition to secular culture and the secular perspective of diversity, a realization that was reinforced throughout my year at GA. At a subsequent meeting, I shared my interview protocols with them and used their feedback to adjust my protocols. Specifically, their feedback encouraged me to ask participants about experiences they had had at the school and probe them about what diversity meant from a biblical perspective. I asked faculty and staff, for example, "What does it mean to approach diversity biblically? Are there any Bible verses or stories that come to mind that could help explain or exemplify the school's approach?" The negotiation process took around six months, and I collected data for a full calendar year after that.

When I began data collection, the head of school thought it was important that I share aspects of my identity with faculty and staff so that they may be more likely to trust me. I learned that most of the researchers with whom the school had previously partnered had more of an insider status because they attended evangelical Christian universities like Liberty University, a school that many GA faculty and staff had themselves attended. Those researchers, Dr. Smith explained, were also not researching topics as sensitive as diversity. Thus, when he introduced me at a faculty/staff meeting, he made sure to mention that I am married and have children, and that I have taught in Christian schools before. Again, I believe that many of GA's faculty and staff assumed that I was more theologically conservative than I am because of my teaching background. Though I didn't try to hide my identity while at GA and always answered questions about where I attended church, I also didn't advertise my religious identity, church membership, or beliefs, especially as I became aware of the stark contrast between my understanding of Christianity and GA's Christianity. I feared being perceived by some as an "internal enemy," to use Antoun's (2001) term, which refers to "non-fundamentalist Christians who claim to be followers of Jesus but accept the norms laid down by the state and other non-religious institutions" and who associate with the wider secular community (p. 56; as cited in Schweber, 2007, p. 62). And some stakeholders at GA did seem to regard me in this way. Early in my data collection, for example, one student confided in me that at least two teachers told him to be careful about what he told me because I was biased against Christian schools. I wonder, though, if other students were likewise warned because the student who told me this happened to be the participant who was most critical of GA's theology and practices, and did not identify as a conservative Christian. I suspect that teachers were trying to dissuade this student from participating in the study or sharing his opinions of the school with me.

Despite my growing disagreement with many conservative Christian beliefs throughout the research process, my shared Christian faith with the study participants allowed me to earnestly participate in prayers with them, which they often did spontaneously before or during interviews. I believe these gestures went a long way in helping participants to feel safe sharing their attitudes and experiences with me. My faith also helped me to be able to recognize and appreciate the sincerity with which many participants approached the study. Numerous participants told me that they believed God had "chosen" me to make their school and other Christian schools better places, and I humbly accepted those statements as great compliments. I also became aware of how much I admired the passion and fervor with which GA stakeholders approached their faith.

My race also helped me negotiate access and shaped my interpretation of and collection of data. I know that my whiteness made me less threatening to the school than had I been a person of color, and I am confident that white participants shared beliefs with me that they wouldn't have shared with a person of color. One white participant, for instance, explained how he felt "white people should marry white people and black people should marry black people." Similarly, a white student shared with me her initial discomfort with more black athletes attending her school. Conversely, I cannot say whether the participants of color would have been more honest or shared different information with me had I been a researcher of color, but I definitely sensed that some participants of color needed to "feel me out" and understand my motivations for research before they shared their attitudes and experiences with me. For example, at the beginning of my interviews with several black parents, I often found myself answering more questions about my racial attitudes than I did with white participants. And several black parents wished to be interviewed with their spouses, so I honored their request.

All of this said, I felt welcomed and accepted at GA. And I am fairly confident that GA's students, faculty, and staff came to see me as an insider or at least as an "observer as participant" (Merriam, 2009, p. 124), even as I was becoming aware of my outsiderness. I say this because I was entrusted with the school's keys and security code. I was invited to sit with the school staff at its graduation ceremony (which I declined), and I was invited on the school's annual summer mission trip to the Dominican Republic (which I also declined). More significantly, people regularly asked me about my life and family.

As other scholars have noted (Peshkin, 1988; Schweber, 2007), when you a spend a year of your life getting to know a community and sharing in their joys and tribulations, writing about that community proves challenging, especially when one's commitment to justice calls one to critically evaluate some of the communities' practices and/or find areas of improvement. I grew close to many people who work at GA, and I am immensely grateful to the school for letting me conduct my research there. Most importantly, I admire them for their willingness to learn from my study. Years later, I still keep in touch with many of the study's participants and share my research with them.

I try throughout this book to present the school's perspective on their practices and situate their practices within the larger educational context and the theological framework they employ. This framing does not give the school a free pass, per se, but rather indicates that many attitudes and practices are not unique to GA and/or make sense within the school's conservative Christian worldview. Many of their struggles are inherent in communities and schools across contexts. In pointing out GA's similarity with other schools, my hope is that readers—professors, educators, school leaders, etc.—can recognize GA's steps and missteps in their own school communities and learn from them.

One early reviewer of this manuscript (when it was in the proposal stages) found the book immensely fascinating but believed I should call out the school's attitudes and practices more blatantly. I was essentially charged with being too neutral. Admittedly, I take the approach of Peshkin (1986, 1988), an ethnographer I greatly admire, and try to tame my subjectivity. Throughout the data collection, analysis, and writing process, I worked hard to become aware of my subjectivity and when and how it was affecting my research process, per Peshkin's (1988) advice. My field notes and analytic memos are littered with brackets containing my opinions and the feelings I experienced as I recorded and analyzed. And I continually wrote and rewrote passages of this book, editing for bias. My hope is that Grace will react similarly to this book as Bethany Baptist Academy did to Alan Peshkin's book about that school: that they will think my portrayal of them is honest and fair (as described in Schweber, 2007), even if seeing some of their missteps or realities in print causes discomfort. As Diangelo (2018) writes of social change, "The key to moving forward is what we do with our discomfort" (p. 14). GA has already demonstrated some of its willingness to learn from its missteps. I also suspect that GA might be proud of some of the very features that I—as an insider-outsider and a more secularly minded Christian and scholar—feel obligated to critique. To be sure, GA's head of school was aware that my position and the lens with which I approached some issues differed from his and the school's. For example, in one of our "member checks" (Merriam, 2009), he acknowledged that the people in "that world you live in" (meaning other scholars and professors) might view GA's stance on LGBTQ issues as bigoted, but that he still believes GA's stance is the right one.

In closing, something that GA staff member, Mr. Reed, said to me in an interview has stayed ever present in my mind as I wrote this book:

> You asked me what's difficult. I think fighting the secular attitude. Culture is hard for us because the secular culture doesn't understand Christians—Number 1: the big picture. Number 2: they don't understand the church. And Number 3: they don't understand the Christian school. They don't understand Christian education. A lot of people, all they're doing is looking in and pointing fingers at us.

My goal in writing this book is not to facilitate the finger pointing. I hope the book will demonstrate that conservative Christian understandings of diversity are more complex than news reports reveal. While some of the assumptions people regularly make about conservative Christian schools will likely be confirmed in this story of a school, I hope that some assumptions will also be debunked. I have tried to capture the perspectives of school stakeholders and their rationales for making the decisions they did. Despite the fact that many would disagree with the rationales presented in this book, myself included, it is important to keep in mind that the people portrayed in this book were thoughtful and their decisions came from a framework and belief system that was really important to them. And few, if any, of the people would describe themselves as racist, bigoted, or discriminatory, even as they participated in and/or promoted marginalizing practices/policies. What's important, as the book's final chapter reveals, is that GA has become intentionally self-reflective of its policies and practices, has learned from my research, has committed to educating themselves, and has made strides in creating a more diverse and inclusive school culture.

Notes

1 The phrases "conservative Christian schools" and "Christian schools" are used interchangeably throughout this book. But the Christian schools to which this book refers generally adhere to conservative Christian theological beliefs, such as an individual relationship with Christ is necessary for salvation (Blosser, 2017; Rose, 1993; Wagner, 1990) and the infallibility of the Bible (Blosser, 2017; Rose, 1993). They are also predominantly white (NCES, 2017). The National Center for Education Statistics (2017) currently classifies conservative Christian schools as those schools holding "membership in at least one of four associations: Accelerated Christian Education, American Association of Christian Schools, Association of Christian Schools International, or Oral Roberts University Education Fellowship" (p. A-3). See also Blosser, 2017, p. 50.
2 Interestingly, that figure refers only to schools holding membership in one of the four associations mentioned earlier. There are another half-million students enrolled in "other affiliated" schools, which refers to those "'other religious' schools not classified as Conservative Christian with membership in at least 1 of 11 associations— Association of Christian Teachers and Schools, Christian Schools International, Evangelical Lutheran Education Association, Friends Council on Education, General Conference of the Seventh-Day Adventist Church, Islamic School League of America, National Association of Episcopal Schools, National Christian School Association, National Society for Hebrew Day Schools, Solomon Schechter Day School Association, Southern Baptist Association of Christian Schools—or indicating membership in 'other religious school associations'" (NCES, 2017, p. A-3). Some of the schools in the "other affiliated" category are likely to share theological beliefs similar to those typically held by conservative Christian schools.
3 For a more detailed literature review of Christian schools, see Blosser, 2017.
4 Scholars such as Blumenfeld (2006) and Burke and Segall (2015) would likely disagree and argue that there are many ways public school acculturates students and teachers into, at the very least, a Christian way of life.
5 Sikkink (1999, 2009) points out that although the majority of conservative Protestants find public schools hostile to their values, this does not mean

that all of them believe in withdrawing them from public schools. Percentages of those favoring withdrawal vary according to the particular stream of conservative Protestantism (i.e., evangelical, fundamentalist, charismatic, Pentecostal).
6 According to conservative Christians, secular humanism "has no absolute values because it has no conception of God" (Flowers, 2005, p. 118). Conservative Christians have latched on to "secular humanism," in particular, because Justice Black claimed it to be a religion in a footnote to the 1961 Supreme Court decision, *Torcaso v. Watkins* (Flowers, 2005; Parsons, 1987). Conservative Christians argue "that if it is unconstitutional to teach traditional religious values, it is equally unconstitutional to teach the religion of secular humanism" (Flowers, 2005, p. 118).
7 In 2006, Florida's Supreme Court ruled that its voucher program was unconstitutional for similar reasons. The Court stated, "This diversion not only reduces money available to the free schools, but also funds private schools that are not 'uniform' when compared with each other or the public system" (Dillon, 2006).
8 Gutmann (1987) claims that the educational standards "essential to democracy" include "teaching religious toleration, mutual respect among races, and those cognitive skills necessary for ensuring all children an adequate education" (p. 118).
9 See Blosser, 2017 for a more detailed review of these studies.
10 Grace Academy is a pseudonym, as are all proper names in the book. In addition, I took extra measures to protect the anonymity of the school and individual participants in the study by changing some details about the school or individual participants that might compromise their or the school's identity with a little research. I did not, however, change any details that would change the analysis presented herein. I also chose not to identify the specific position for most of GA's faculty and staff except when absolutely necessary in order to protect participant's individual identities. Likewise, because only five members of GA's faculty/staff identified as persons of color, I chose not to identify the race of any faculty/staff member in order to protect the participants' identities within the school.
11 See the appendix for more details about sampling criteria and research methods.
12 I also briefly describe the research site and methods in Blosser (2017).
13 See the appendix for a detailed description of the sampling criteria or Blosser (2017) for an abbreviated list.

References

American Bar Association. (2017). *Brief of Amicus Curiae ethics & religious liberty commission in support of petitioner*. Retrieved from www.americanbar.org/content/dam/aba/publications/supreme_court_preview/briefs_2016_2017/15-577_Amicus_pet_EthicsReligiousLibertyCommission.authcheckdam.pdf

Anti-Defamation League. (2012). *School vouchers: The wrong choice for public education*. Retrieved from www.adl.org/. . . ./School-Vouchers-docx.pdf

Antoun, R. (2001). *Understanding fundamentalism: Christian, Islamic, and Jewish movements*. Lanham, MD: Rowman & Littlefield.

Associated Press. (2017, October 1). Transgender teen says he was kicked out of Christian school. *Fox News Network*. Retrieved from www.foxnews.com/us/transgender-teen-says-he-was-kicked-out-of-christian-school

Association of Christian Schools International (ACSI). (2014). *Services*. Retrieved from www.acsiglobal.org/services

Bacon, P., Jr., & Thomson-DeVeaux, A. (2018, March 2). How Trump and race are splitting evangelicals. *Five Thirty Eight*. Retrieved from https://fivethirtyeight.com/features/how-trump-and-race-are-splitting-evangelicals/

Bechard, B. (2018). NC private schools receiving vouchers: A study of the curriculum. *The League of Women Voters of North Carolina*. Retrieved from https://lwvnc.org/wp-content/uploads/2018/04/Voucher-Report-7.2-1.pdf

Beckford, J. A. (1973). Religious organization. *Current Sociology*, 21(7), 7–104.

Bendery, J. (2014, July 21). Obama signs executive order on LGBT job discrimination. *The Huffington Post*. Retrieved from www.huffingtonpost.com/2014/07/21/obama-gay-rights_n_5605482.html

Berg, T. C. (2003). Vouchers and religious schools: The new constitutional questions. University *of Cincinnati Law Review*, 72(1), 151–222.

Blosser, A. H. (2017). Considerations for addressing diversity in Christian schools. In D. B. Hiatt-Michael (Ed.), *Family and community engagement in faith-based schools* (pp. 33–55). Charlotte, NC: Information Age Publishing, Inc.

Blumenfeld, W. J. (2006). Christian privilege and the promotion of "secular" and not-so "secular" mainline Christianity in public schooling and in the larger society. *Equity and Excellence in Education*, 39(3), 195–210.

Blumenfeld, S. (2012). Secular humanism: American's establishment of religion. *The New American*. Retrieved from www.thenewamerican.com/reviews/opinion/item/11549-secular-humanism-americas-establishment-of-religion

Bob Jones University v. United States. 461 (U.S.). 574.(1983).

Brown, E. (2011). "It's about race . . . no, it isn't!" Negotiating race and social class: Youth identities at Anderson school in 2005. In D. T. Slaughter-Defoe, H. C. Stevenson, E. G. Arrington, & D. J. Johnson (Eds.), *Black educational choice: Assessing the private and public alternatives to traditional K–12 public schools* (pp. 28–48). Santa Barbara, CA: ABC-CLIO, LLC.

Burke, K. J., & Segall, A. (2015). Teaching as Jesus making: The hidden curriculum of Christ in schooling. *Teachers College Record*, 117(3), 1–27.

Burton, T. I. (2018, October 3). White evangelicals are the only religious group to support Trump. *Vox*. Retrieved from www.vox.com/identities/2018/10/3/17929696/white-evangelicals-prri-poll-trump-presidency-support

Candal, C. S., & Glenn, C. L. (2012). Race relations in an evangelical and a Catholic urban high school. *Journal of School Choice*, 6(1), 82–103.

Chou, D., & others. (1982). Discriminatory religious schools and tax exempt status. *Commission on Civil Rights*. Retrieved from https://files.eric.ed.gov/fulltext/ED228712.pdf

Christian Schools International (CSI). (2014). *Our services*. Retrieved from www.csionline.org/home

Coburn, C. E. (2001). Collective sensemaking about reading: How teachers mediate reading policy in their professional communities. *Educational Evaluation and Policy Analysis*, 23(2), 145–170.

Coburn, C. E. (2004). Beyond decoupling: Rethinking the relationship between the institutional environment and the classroom. *Sociology of Education*, 77(3), 211–244.

Council for American Private Education (CAPE). (2014). *Facts and studies*. Retrieved from www.capenet.org/facts.html

Council for American Private Education (CAPE). (2017). *Facts and studies*. Retrieved from www.capenet.org/facts.html

Diangelo, R. (2018). *White fragility: Why it's so hard for white people to talk about racism*. Boston, MA: Beacon Press.

Dillon, S. (2006, January 6). Florida supreme court blocks school vouchers. *The New York Times*. Retrieved from www.nytimes.com/2006/01/06/national/06florida.html?pagewanted=print&_r=0

DiMaggio, P. (1998). The relevance of organizational theory to the study of religion. In N. J. Demerath III, P. D. Hall, T. Schmitt, & R. H. Williams (Eds.), *Sacred companies: Organizational aspects of religion and religious aspects of organizations* (pp. 7–23). New York, NY: Oxford UP.

Dunlap, E. D., Jr. (2014, August 22). Court rules voucher program unconstitutional. *North Carolina School Boards Association*. Retrieved from www.ncsba.org

Education Commission of the States. (2017). *50-state comparison: Vouchers*. Retrieved from www.ecs.org/50-state-comparison-vouchers/

Evans, A. E. (2007). School leaders and their sensemaking about race and demographic change. Educational *Administration Quarterly, 43*(2), 159–188.

Finke, R., & Stark, R. (2005). *The churching of America, 1776–2005: Winners and losers in our religious economy*. New Brunswick, NJ: Rutgers University Press.

Flowers, R. B. (2005). *That godless court?* (2nd ed.). Louisville, KY: Westminster John Knox Press.

Godwin, K., Ausbrooks, C., & Martinez, V. (2001). Teaching tolerance in public and private schools. *The Phi Delta Kappan, 82*(7), 542–546.

Godwin, R. K., Godwin, J. W., & Martinez-Ebers, V. (2004). Civic socialization in public and fundamentalist schools. *Social Science Quarterly, 85*(5), 1097–1111.

Goldstein, J. (2004). Making sense of distributed leadership: The case of peer assistance and review. *Educational Evaluation and Policy Analysis, 26*(2), 173–197.

Green, E. L. (2017, June 10). To understand Betsy DeVos' educational views, view her education. *The New York Times*. Retrieved from www.nytimes.com/2017/06/10/us/politics/betsy-devos-private-schools-choice.html

Green, J. (2006). Christ-centered, diverse, and academically excellent. *American Educational History Journal, 33*(1), 89–95.

Gutmann, A. (1987). *Democratic education*. Princeton, NJ: Princeton UP.

Gutmann, A. (1999). *Democratic education: With a new preface and epilogue*. Princeton, NJ: Princeton UP.

Helms, A. D. (2016, April 8). Praying for options: Religious schools dominate NC voucher program. *Charlotte Observer*. Retrieved from www.charlotteobserver.com/news/local/education/article70759617.html

Jones, S. (2013, December 11). Equal education: N.C. Christian school rejects vouchers after discrimination fight. *Wall of Separation*. Retrieved from www.au.org/blogs/wall-of-separation/equal-education-nc-christian-school-rejects-vouchers-after-discrimination

Katz, L. L. (1999). In pursuit of the multicultural curriculum. *Independent School, 58*(2), 31–36.

Levinson, M., & Levinson, S. (2003). "Getting religion": Religion, diversity, and community in public and private schools. In S. Levinson (Ed.), *Wrestling with diversity* (pp. 90–123). Durham, NC: Duke University Press.

Mawdsley, R. D., & Russo, C. J. (2013). Vouchers and religious schools: Why some religious schools may refuse to participate. *Journal of Catholic Education*, 6(3), 362–371.

Merriam, S. B. (2009). *Qualitative research: A guide to design and implementation*. San Francisco, CA: Jossey-Bass.

Miller, L. (2012, June 22). Why are evangelicals supporting immigration reform? *The Washington Post*. Retrieved from www.washingtonpost.com/national/on-faith/why-are-evangelicals-supporting-immigration-reform/2012/06/22/gJQAn4JNvV_story.html

National Center for Education Statistics (NCES). (2017). *Characteristics of private schools in the United States: Results from the 2015–16 Private school universe survey*. Retrieved from https://nces.ed.gov/pubs2017/2017073.pdf

Nevin, D., & Bills, R. E. (1976). *The schools that fear built: Segregationist academies in the South*. Washington, DC: Acropolis Books Ltd.

Parsons, P. F. (1987). *Inside America's Christian schools*. Macon, GA: Mercer University Press.

Patton, M. Q. (2002). *Qualitative research and evaluation methods* (3rd ed.). Thousand Oaks, CA: Sage.

Peshkin, A. (1986). *God's choice: The total world of a fundamentalist Christian school*. Chicago, IL: University of Chicago Press.

Peshkin, A. (1988). In search of subjectivity—One's own. *Educational Researcher*, 17(7), 17–21.

Pew Forum. (2007). *Changing faiths: Latinos and the transformation of American religion*. Retrieved from www.pewforum.org/Changing-Faiths-Latinos-and-the-Transformation-of-American-Religion.aspx

Pew Research Center. (2015). America's changing religious landscape. *Pew Research Center*. Retrieved from www.pewforum.org/2015/05/12/americas-changing-religious-landscape/

Phillippo, K., Brown, E. L., & Blosser, A. (2018). Making sense of student-teacher relationships: Teacher educator and candidate engagement with the relational practices of teaching. *Action in Teacher Education*, 40(2), 169–185.

Prangley, E. (2014, January 24). Voucher schools provide choice, except when they don't. *American Association of University Women*. Retrieved from www.aauw.org/2014/01/24/vouchers-and-national-school-choice-week/

Pratt, M. G. (2000). Building an ideological fortress: The role of spirituality, encapsulation and sensemaking. *Studies in Cultures, Organizations, and Societies*, 6, 35–69.

Rizga, K. (2017). Betsy Devos wants to use America's schools to build "God's kingdom." *Mother Jones*. Retrieved from www.motherjones.com/politics/2017/01/betsy-devos-christian-schools-vouchers-charter-education-secretary/

Rose, S. (1988). *Keeping them out of the hands of Satan: Evangelical schooling in America*. New York, NY: Routledge, Chapman and Hall, Inc.

Rose, S. (1993). Christian fundamentalism and education in the United States. In M. Marty & R. S. Appleby (Eds.), *Fundamentalisms and society* (pp. 452–489). Chicago, IL: University of Chicago Press.

Rury, J. L. (2016). *Education and social change: Contours in the history of American schooling* (5th ed.). New York, NY: Routledge.

Russo, C. J., Soules, K. E., Newman, A. C., & Douglas, S. L. (2018). Private religious schools. In M. D. Waggoner & N. C. Walker (Eds.), *Oxford handbook of religion and American education* (pp. 169–188). New York, NY: Oxford UP.

Schweber, S. (2007). Donning wigs, divining feelings, and other dilemmas of doing research in devoutly religious contexts. *Qualitative Inquiry*, *13*(1), 58–84.

Schweber, S., & Irwin, R. (2003). "Especially special": Learning about Jews in a fundamentalist Christian school. *Teachers College Record*, *105*(9), 1693–1719.

Sikkink, D. (1999). The social sources of alienation from public schools. *Social Forces*, *78*(1), 51–86.

Sikkink, D. (2009). Conservative protestants, schooling, and democracy. In S. Brint & J. Reith (Eds.), *Evangelicals and democracy in America* (pp. 276–303). New York, NY: Russell Sage.

Spillane, J. P., Diamond, J. B., Burch, P., Hallett, T., Jita, L., & Zoltners, J. (2002). Managing in the middle: School leaders and the enactment of accountability policy. *Educational Policy*, *16*(5), 731–762.

Spillane, J. P., Reiser, B. J., & Reimer, T. (2002). Policy implementation and cognition: Reframing and refocusing implementation research. *Review of Educational Research*, *72*(3), 387–431.

Stevens, M. L. (2002). The organizational vitality of conservative Protestantism. In M. Lounsbury & M. J. Ventresca (Eds.), *Social structure and organizations revisited* (Vol. 19, pp. 337–360). Bingley, UK: Emerald Group Publishing Limited.

Stitzlein, S. M. (2008). Private interests, public necessity: Responding to sexism in Christian schools. *Educational Studies*, *43*(1), 45–57.

Strauss, V. (2013, March 26). School vouchers: Still a bad idea despite Indiana court ruling. *The Washington Post*. Retrieved from www.washingtonpost.com/blogs/answer-sheet/wp/2013/03/26/school-vouchers-still-a-bad-idea-despite-indiana-court-ruling/

Strauss, V. (2017, June 26). Will the Supreme Court's Trinity decision lead to the spread of school voucher programs? *The Washington Post*. Retrieved from www.washingtonpost.com/news/answer-sheet/wp/2017/06/26/will-the-supreme-courts-trinity-decision-lead-to-the-spread-of-school-voucher-programs/?utm_term=.cc16f1cee5df

Strauss, V., Douglas-Gabriel, D., & Balingit, M. (2018, February 13). Devos seeks cuts from education department to support school choice. *Washington Post*. Retrieved from www.washingtonpost.com/news/education/wp/2018/02/12/devos-seeks-massive-cuts-from-education-department-to-support-school-choice/?utm_term=.54fbac7a794b

Wagner, L. (2013, December 9). Anti-gay Christian School won't accept school vouchers. *NC Policy Watch*. Retrieved from http://pulse.ncpolicywatch.org/2013/12/09/anti-gay-christian-school-wont-accept-school-vouchers/

Wagner, L. (2014, February 26). Discriminatory practices in North Carolina's prospective voucher schools. *NC Policy Watch*. Retrieved from www.ncpolicywatch.com/2014/02/26/discriminatory-practices-abound-in-north-carolinas-prospective-voucher-schools/

Wagner, M. B. (1990). *God's schools: Choice and compromise in American Society*. New Brunswick, NJ: Rutgers University Press.

Wagner, M. B. (1997). Generic conservative Christianity: The demise of denominationalism in Christian schools. *Journal for the Scientific Study of Religion*, 36(1), 13–24.

Whetten, D. A. (2006). Albert and Whetten revisited: Strengthening the concept of organizational identity. *Journal of Management Inquiry*, 15(3), 219–223.

Weick, K. E. (1995). *Sensemaking in organizations*. Thousand Oaks, CA: Sage Publications.

Yeakley, R. (2011, February 15). Evangelical churches still growing, mainline Protestantism in decline. *Huffington Post*. Retrieved from www.huffingtonpost.com/2011/02/15/report-us-churches-contin_n_823701.html

Zehr, M. A. (2005). Evangelical schools represent the fastest growing sector of private schools. *Education Week*, 25(14), 31–34.

Zelman v. Simmons-Harris, 536 U.S. (2002).

Note: I exclude references that might in any way compromise the identity of the school.

2 Grace Academy
Unapologetically Christian

Grace Academy (GA) is a college-preparatory, evangelical Christian school located in a small city in a southern state.[1] At the time of the study (2013–2014), the school enrolled around 1,000 students from kindergarten to 12th grade. Four principals (three white males and a white female) and the white male head of school made up the school's leadership team. The head of school reported to a board that was predominantly composed of members of the church with which the school was affiliated, though it had recently added two members from the general public. The board generally supported the head of school's decisions and granted him a lot of autonomy in the daily operations of the school.

In 2013–2014, about 9% of students identified as students of color, and over half of those students identified as African American.[2] GA had been recently turned down when it applied to become a College Board member school because its demographics did not reflect the ethnic diversity of the city in which it was located, Cedar Ridge.[3] Yearly tuition ranged from approximately $8,500 to $10,000, depending on the grade level. Roughly a quarter of students received some sort of financial aid.[4] The school employed approximately 23 full-time staff, 84 full-time faculty, and 9 part-time faculty/staff. Approximately 4% of staff and faculty identified as persons of color. All of the teachers were state certified, and over half held advanced degrees. The average tenure for teachers at Grace Academy was 14 years.

At the time of the study, Cedar Ridge was (and still is) a small city.[5] About half of Cedar Ridge's population was white. A third of the population was black. About 9% was Hispanic and about 6% was Asian. The remaining 2% of the population identified as multiracial, American Indian, Hawaiian/Pacific Islander, or other. In 2014, the average median family income for the city was around $44,000, which was slightly lower than the state's average. In general, there were pockets of extreme wealth throughout the city, and the city was geographically segregated by race. A majority of its public schools classified as Title 1 schools, meaning they had high percentages of low-income students. Cedar Ridge also contained a lot of private schools for its size: three prominent conservative

Christian K–12 schools, a mainline Christian K–8 school, a Catholic K–8 school, a secular K–12 school, and a school exclusively for students with special needs. Grace Academy was the largest of all of the private schools.

Grace was not established as a white flight school after integration, which distinguishes it from many southern Christian schools (Blosser, 2017; Chou et al., 1982; Flowers, 2005; Gutmann, 1987; Nevin & Bills, 1976; Parsons, 1987; Rose, 1988, 1993). Grace began in the 1970s as a church preschool program. In the early 1970s, Grace added their elementary program. A decade later, it was serving students through the sixth grade and merged with another area Christian school that was serving students through high school. Grace Academy graduated its first class in the 1980s.

Grace Academy's campus was impressive. The school's campus consisted of over 25 acres, and included an Olympic-sized swimming pool, tennis courts, two basketball gyms, several athletic fields, a weight room and physical therapy room, several playgrounds, a performing arts center, music and dance practice rooms, approximately 60 classrooms, 3 computer labs, and a large auditorium. Classrooms were well-lit, orderly, and nicely decorated with materials relevant to the subject being taught.

The school also had an impressive academic record. In addition to a competitive admissions process requiring tests, interviews, and recommendations, the school avowed that their college-preparatory curriculum began in kindergarten. The high school offered numerous honors and advanced placement (AP) courses, and almost three quarters of students took AP courses. Over 99% of graduating seniors from Grace attended college, and the school boasted that its students were awarded an average of 3.5 million dollars in merit-based college scholarships each year. Students attended a range of schools from community colleges to Ivy League universities, but the majority of students attended four-year state universities or liberal arts colleges.

Grace Academy was affiliated with a conservative denomination and church, even though its student population was ecumenical. The basic tenets of the school's theology as stated in its Statement of Faith centered on the infallibility and authority of the Bible, the Triune God, the need for salvation, the resurrection, and the indwelling of the Holy Spirit. Accordingly, GA's "mission [was] to partner with parents and provide students a biblically-centered, college-preparatory education so that they [could] follow Christ and transform the world" (Blosser, 2017, p. 40). Likewise, its vision statement centered on living out God's truth. And its Statement of Purpose indicated the school's desire to help each student achieve salvation through faith in Christ.

In both attitude and practice, GA was "unapologetically Christian," to use the words of the school's admissions director. That is, GA's most salient characteristic was its conservative Christian ideology,[6] and that ideology shaped its policies, practices, and curriculum (Blosser, 2017). Several school stakeholders described GA as a Christian "bubble," and they proudly viewed themselves as distinct from or set apart from secular culture and the world. I regularly heard statements such as this one from Mr. Tate, a teacher at GA,

> I think Christianity is a pretty radical worldview. If I become so much like the culture that you can't tell the difference between me and somebody that doesn't believe Jesus resurrected from the dead, then what am I doing? So I don't think assimilating to the culture and becoming just like it is where I want to go.

GA's desire to resist the ways of secular culture, then, shaped much of the decision making.

Further, GA's primary concern was producing strong Christians who led a Christian life. It was a regular practice of teachers at the school to begin class with a short devotional reading and/or a prayer. And classrooms were often decorated with Bible passages and other Christian symbols, such as crosses, the Christian flag, and images of Jesus. All students attended a weekly chapel service that included a praise band and Christian speakers. And both students and faculty were generally comfortable talking about their faith and spiritual practices. I frequently observed discussions of faith in classes and in student speeches or presentations.

Several school documents also defined what GA considered to be a Christian lifestyle. For faculty and staff, the school's employment contract included prohibitions against drinking, smoking, viewing pornography, premarital sex, extramarital sex, and participating in "homosexual activity" (GA Employment Contract, 2013). Faculty were also expected to regularly attend and financially contribute to a church whose beliefs align with GA's. Moreover, they were expected to resolve possible legal disputes privately or in consultation with Christian mediators. Similarly, students were supposed to treat their bodies as "temple[s]" with respect to exercise, eating, and the choices they make regarding sexual activity, drugs, alcohol, etc. (GA Student Outcomes, 2012; GA Student Handbook, 2014), and they were expected to be properly groomed. The school's dress code allowed K–4 students to wear shorts, but they had to be no shorter than two-inches above the knees. Students were not allowed to wear ripped clothing or any clothes containing symbols that could have "occult" associations, like the peace sign. In addition, there were strict rules about hairstyles, clothes, makeup, and piercings. For example, boys had to always tuck in their shirts and were not allowed to wear earrings or have long hair, and girls could not wear tight clothing.

In accordance with the school's ideology, and consistent with other studies of conservative Christian schools (e.g., Parsons, 1987; Peshkin, 1986; Rose, 1988; Wagner, 1990), GA's culture was also defined by an emphasis on authority. Throughout GA's literature were statements about authority. GA students were taught to recognize that ultimate authority rests in God and Christ, but that they should also respect those individuals in the earthly realm who have God-granted authority over them—namely, parents and teachers. Further, deference to authority was not just something reflected in GA's documents, but it was also something I observed. GA students were incredibly respectful of adults and were well-mannered. I rarely observed behavioral disruptions in class. Teachers communicated their authority in the classroom by wearing microphones and dressing professionally. There was also a clear chain of command between faculty/staff and the administration. Faculty and staff typically accepted the decisions of the administration with little questioning or discussion, even privately among themselves. Accordingly, none of the faculty/staff meetings I observed included time for faculty and staff to discuss or ask questions about the topic at hand.

The school saw itself in partnership with parents to educate students in Christ and help them develop a Christian worldview. Not surprisingly, then, GA parents were quite involved in their children's education. Parents felt assured that they could contact their child's teacher at any time, and many did. Parents were also giving of their time and money. At almost every event I observed, there were numerous parent volunteers. And the parents I interviewed were attracted to the discipline and structure GA provided, as well as the Christian values it instilled, regardless of their own religious beliefs. They acknowledged that their children were sheltered at GA and were happy about it. Parents also believed that GA was academically superior to public school.

Moreover, many of the people I interviewed described the Grace community as a family. I often heard claims such as, "All of us will bend over backwards for each other" (Mrs. Dillard, a teacher), and, indeed, I witnessed an incredible amount of trust and support for one another. It was not uncommon for a teacher to ask students questions about their lives outside of school or to pray for something going on in a particular student's life. To illustrate the closeness of the school, when a staff member's granddaughter was diagnosed with a life-threatening illness, the Grace community rallied around him by posting ribbons on classroom doors in honor of the girl, by holding fundraisers for her treatment, and by praying for her regularly. I was also surprised that at least three administrators and several teachers visited a GA student in the hospital after the student had a heart attack. Likewise, there were no locks on any of the lockers because students trusted each other not to invade their privacy or steal their belongings. "Family" was also a literal descriptor of the school, as many of the school stakeholders were related. During the course of my study, there were at least six employee couples at the school, and many faculty and staff had children, grandchildren, or other family members attending the school. Some of the school's faculty/staff were also former students.

GA high school students were smart and articulate and exhibited a lot of school pride. Students came together to cheer for their school. Sporting events united the student body as students dressed up, painted their bodies, chanted, and cheered for GA. During homecoming, each grade level in the high school competed to see which class was the most spirited. They decorated the hallways, built floats for a parade, and performed skits. There was a definite sense of familiarity among the students, which stemmed from the fact that a large majority of each class had been going to school together since kindergarten.

Grace Academy's Diversity Initiative

Organizational sensemaking is ongoing process, but it also happens in response to interruptions in the status quo (Weick, 1995). GA experienced a major interruption when a new head of school, Dr. Smith, arrived in the late 2000s, replacing the retired and much beloved previous head of school of over 30 years. Under the leadership of the prior head of school, GA had waiting lists for almost every grade, and it had boasted its selectivity. By the time of Dr. Smith's arrival, that had begun to change. While enrollment remained relatively steady, there were waiting lists for only a few grades, and much to the chagrin of veteran faculty and staff, GA couldn't afford to be as selective as it once was. Dr. Smith had to confront this changing reality upon his arrival. In addition, Dr. Smith came to GA valuing diversity and was eager to address it. When Dr. Smith interviewed at GA, he recognized the school's lack of racial diversity and told the board he believed GA needed to become more diverse. He told them that he felt it was sending the wrong message that the school's only black staff were serving lunch and picking up trash. And helping schools become more diverse was a skill in his repertoire. Prior to arriving at Grace, Dr. Smith was the head of school at a Christian school in the North, where he had worked to increase its racial and ethnic diversity. The board supported Dr. Smith when he proposed GA's diversity initiative.

Dr. Smith said he cared about diversity because of an experience in his personal life. He told me that due to the demographics of the community in which he used to live, his daughter didn't see a black person for the first time until she was three years old and that made him realize he wanted her to grow up in a more diverse environment. Already in school administration at that time, it was at that point that he began more ardently caring about the demographics of the schools where he worked and where his daughter attended.

Upon Dr. Smith's arrival, GA was also in the process of becoming accredited by the Association of Christian Schools International (ACSI),[7] creating another change in the status quo for GA. As part of the accreditation process, ACSI examined GA's policies and procedures, and it determined that one of its three major recommendations for GA was the development of a diversity statement that aligned with the school's values and ideology, and reflected a desire for a more ethnically diverse staff and student body (GA Accreditation Report, 2010).

These two events prompted organizational sensemaking about diversity across two levels. Initially, the administration had to figure out how they wanted to address diversity at GA, which meant formalizing the school's efforts via a strategic plan and the development of an official diversity statement. Then GA faculty and staff had to figure out what the new initiative meant for their daily practices. I learned in interviews and casual conversations with Dr. Smith and the school's four principals that there was a lot of debate among them over how to develop a diversity statement that aligned with the school's values per ACSI's recommendation. It is important to note here that when people make sense of something they "plac[e] new information into preexisting cognitive frameworks, also called 'worldviews' or 'working knowledge' by some theorists" (Coburn, 2005, p. 478). The predominant worldview shaping administrators' sensemaking about diversity, then, was a conservative Christian one. The administration decided that GA's diversity efforts had to be distinctively Christian, because in their view, secular culture had not approached diversity in the way God would desire (Blosser, 2017). Principal Barnes explained their thinking about the diversity initiative:

> We are a Christian school, but by and large, we don't live in a Christian culture anymore. So those two realities mean that our school won't reflect the culture. So on some level it's not going to reflect the culture. On some level, we don't want to reflect the culture.

The administration's sensemaking at this point led them to conclude that "doing diversity" at GA should look different than it would at public or secular private schools and that any diversity efforts should complement the school's goal of building strong Christians.

The administration's first action was to develop a diversity goal as part of the school's five-year strategic plan. The goal, which was to faithfully integrate diversity into the culture of the school, reflected the administration's desire to make diversity fit the school's mission by tying diversity to spiritual formation. The school's plan was to develop a Christian environment that would enable students to successfully navigate both conflicting Christian viewpoints and a rapidly changing secular culture. Added to that description was an assertion that the school's environment must encourage demographics that reflect the ethnic diversity of the US (GA Strategic Plan, 2010). Essentially, then, GA's diversity goal was concerned with both preparing students for the secular and Christian circles in which they would find themselves after high school and the creation of a racially and ethnically diverse environment.

The school administration developed strategies in an effort to meet their goal. Most of the strategies were designed to help its students grow spiritually, like increasing the opportunities for mission and evangelism, but two of them were designed to foster diversity within the school. Specifically, GA sought 1) to develop means of outreach to under-represented populations at the school and 2) to use a biblical framework to attain a diverse staff and student body that would encourage students to better understand and work with individuals from diverse cultures (GA Strategic Plan, 2010). The second strategy, in particular, because of its reliance on a biblical framework, uniquely reflected the administration's sense-making in that they planned to recruit diverse individuals in ways that were compatible with the school's conservative Christian ideology.

After developing the diversity goal in the strategic plan, the administration also developed GA's first diversity statement. The finalized statement was officially presented to the faculty in the fall of 2013. Dr. Smith was proud of this statement and told me numerous times how he felt GA's diversity statement was unique for its truly "biblical approach" to diversity. Using theological tenets and scripture as tools for their sense-making, the administration decided that GA's diversity statement needed to reflect God's truth, a notion they deemed absent from secular conceptions of diversity. Principal Westerly explained his view of the secular understanding of diversity:

> We're not looking for multiculturalism in the sense that secularism does. [. . .] And in secularism, there is only a rationale, an epistemology for diversity . . . because everything is culturally constructed. Gender is a cultural construction. Race is a cultural construction. It's all about diversity and their culture. There's no such thing as truth in post modern time.

Principal Westerly, then, believed that from a secular point of view, facets of identity were culturally constructed.

In conservative Christianity, conversely, there was absolute truth, which had implications for how one understood diversity. Moreover, secular culture's disregard for truth claims directly contrasted GA's vision statement concerning living out God's truth. Principal Westerly explained how the Christian belief in absolute truth offered a different conception of diversity than secularism:

> I think the beauty that the circle of Christianity brings is it asserts without ambiguity certain truth claims about origins that bring unity to our diversity. So, if we deal with parents who are different skin pigmentation or cultural background, we can at once recognize some level of diversity in the culture, but we recognize that we come from one source. We are of Adam. We are image bearers of God.

From his perspective then, a conservative Christian conception of diversity maintained that more important than recognizing the characteristics that differentiated people was recognizing the characteristic that united them: God the Father. GA's diversity statement[8] was crafted to reflect this notion, though it emphasized Christ, not God, as the unifying force. It used the following passage from Colossians 3:11 as its premise: "Here there is no Gentile or Jew, circumcised or uncircumcised, barbarian, Scythian, slave or free, but Christ is all, and is in all." It stated that GA sought a racially, ethnically, and socioeconomically diverse student body and staff that reflected the broader world in which they minister.[9] It claimed that the school welcomed students with learning differences while it remained committed to academic rigor. Further, the statement claimed that the school did not purport to set or fulfill targets for percentages of diverse students or staff, but rather to create a climate where students can appreciate and celebrate each other's God-created differences. The final few sentences of the statement reemphasized the school's biblical approach to diversity in that the school's interest was in cultivating unity in Christ. It stated that GA "intentionally" desired for every member of the school community (parents, students, and staff) to feel that their God-given culture is respected.

Dr. Smith felt that the Colossians passage perfectly captured the idea of unity in diversity. In addition to the statement's emphasis on unity, the statement also indicated which facets of identity were included in the school's definition of diversity and, by default, which facets were not. The school sought diversity in terms of race, ethnicity, socioeconomic status, and ability, but not in terms of religion or sexual orientation. Religion and sexual orientation were not, according to GA's theology, differences "created" by God (Blosser, 2017). Mrs. Flynn, a teacher, perhaps explained it best in her interpretation of the school's diversity statement,

> They're (the administration) talking strictly about ethnic diversity, racial diversity. They're not getting into the things that go against the biblical principle: homosexuality. That statement does not include that, if you believe like the Bible says. [. . .] I don't think that they're going to be into bringing in two moms to show how two moms can be parents in a family.

The administration's sensemaking, then, led to a construction of diversity that determined the kinds of diverse staff and students GA sought. The statement also specified that doing diversity at GA concerned two overarching efforts: 1) the recruitment of a diverse staff and student body and 2) the creation of an environment in which students learned to celebrate diversity. The second effort involved teaching students about diversity via curriculum, programs, policies, and practices.

As school leaders introduce new initiatives, they "provid[e] the overarching interpretative frame that teachers adopt as they construct their understanding of the approach" (Coburn, 2005, p. 494). School leaders are also "gatekeepers," wherein they get to choose which parts of environmental messages get emphasized and which do not (Coburn, 2005, p. 490). At GA, school leaders provided a conservative Christian frame through which other faculty and staff could make sense of the school's diversity initiative.

Colorblindness

GA faculty and staff used scripture and other conservative Christian theological concepts to make sense of the school's diversity initiative and figure out what it meant for their daily attitudes and practices. To make sense of the initiative's central focus on unity in diversity, for instance, Mr. Lang, a high school teacher, referred to a scripture passage (i.e., 1 Cor. 12: 12–27) about how each part of the body was uniquely created for a different function but they worked together as one. Another teacher, Mr. Vance, told me that the notion of the Trinity helped him understand unity in diversity. As he explained, "The Trinity is the perfect representation of diversity for Christians because the Trinity consists of three distinct bodies that combine in perfect unity." Often referring to the Colossians passage that framed the school's diversity initiative, faculty and staff also generally agreed that achieving unity in diversity required colorblindness concerning racial differences because God did not see differences between people (i.e., "here there is no Gentile or Jew"). Belief in colorblindness was, in fact, the most prominent outcome of faculty and staff sensemaking about GA's diversity initiative, appearing as a theme in 12 faculty and staff interviews.

The rationale for colorblindness is that recognizing someone's race and treating them differently as a result creates division (Blosser, 2017; Harris, 2012; Yancey, 2006). Those practicing colorblindness in schools or elsewhere tend to favor policies and practices that emphasize equal treatment over equitable treatment. They believe that race doesn't matter and choose not to acknowledge it. The following statements are representative of the kind of colorblind attitudes I heard from faculty and staff:

> I don't see any difference. I really don't. We were all created, and I was just thinking the other day, the color of the skin . . . why is that any different than the color of our hair? I just can't, I just don't understand. . . . I just don't see the difference.
> (Mrs. Willis, a high school teacher)

> "Diversity to me is basically not seeing diversity" (Mr. Sweeney, a middle school teacher).

I both heard such affirmations of colorblindness and observed colorblind actions. Specifically, I observed how few courses or activities emphasized cultural differences, even at times one would normally anticipate their emphasis. For example, GA did not celebrate Martin Luther King Jr. Day,[10] even though some faculty and staff seemed to believe he promoted a Christian conception of colorblindness[11] (Blosser, 2017). The school also did not have diversity activities for Black History Month (Blosser, 2017). But this approach is consistent with a commitment to colorblindness. The following comment from Mr. Gill, a middle school teacher, demonstrates such logic: "Everybody should be equal and not be treated differently. As such, I don't like . . . for Black History month, I don't do special things." He elaborated, "Celebrate our differences . . . but don't notice them."

Colorblindness is a widely embraced model for dealing with racial issues among white, evangelical Christians (Emerson & Smith, 2000; Harris, 2012; Yancey, 2006). It is compatible with conservative Christian ideology, as it can be theologically justified. Yancey (2006) explains, "Christianity is a religion in which superficial qualities such as a person's race become unimportant when we are confronted with the eternal significance of Christ. From an eternal perspective, it is definitely Christian to use the colorblindness model" (p. 39). And GA viewed colorblindness that way as well. From their perspective, one did not need to pay special attention to people's differences in order to celebrate diversity; rather, celebrating diversity meant recognizing the power of Christ to unite the many different people who follow him (Blosser, 2017).

Evangelical Christians support colorblindness because they believe that drawing attention to differences creates division, not the unity in Christ they desire. Mr. Gill's attitude toward diversity illustrated such a premise:

> So, it's (diversity) not something to be avoided, but yet at the same time you celebrate it too much, and you make it the whole point of your course, the whole point of your school, the whole point of your life, [then] it becomes divisive and people want to defend themselves and their viewpoints and their tribe.

Emerson and Smith (2000) explain that evangelicals see the race problem as a "relational proble[m] between a few sinful individuals" (p. 80). They believe that institutions make the race problem to be more than an individual problem and maintain that "if these institutions would leave the race issue alone, the race problem would nearly disappear" (Emerson & Smith, 2000, p. 80). In particular, white evangelicals tend to blame the government for creating a race problem (Emerson & Smith, 2000). Mr. Reed, a staff member, expressed his view that government regulations about diversity had made things worse: "They make laws to dictate diversity and it's just putting a bigger wedge in, making a worse problem out of it." Mrs. Harper, another GA staff member, held a similar attitude and believed that diversity problems would work themselves out naturally if the government stayed out of it:

> I think politicians have kind of gotten in the way to be very honest. I think there's been too much "these people are different, and let's see how we can make them the same." If you let nature take its course, I think people would handle that.

Letting nature take its course is an appealing belief to white advocates of colorblindness because it often requires no drastic change in diversity practices for them. And some teachers didn't see much effort from GA to become more diverse. Teachers Mr. Baxter and Mr. Armstrong noted, for instance,

> I don't see anything that is deliberate, that is purposeful, that is moving us to . . . I don't know that we're looking for a more diversified school. —Mr. Baxter
>
> I feel like there's not much effort to have more African American people here. —Mr. Armstrong.

Moreover, a colorblind perspective may have even prevented school stakeholders from recognizing issues related to diversity. As Principal Kline said to me, "Really and truly I don't see us as having any diversity issues that are negative. So maybe it will be good to have a study like this because it will help us to see if there is an issue."

Colorblindness is also anchored in political conservatism (Harris, 2012; Yancey, 2006), which fit the political ethos of GA. Advocates of colorblindness generally reject laws and policies that grant special consideration to people because of their race, like Affirmative Action, because they deem them unfair, especially to white people (Emerson & Smith, 2000; Yancey, 2006). The alternative to considering race in admissions or hiring decisions, they maintain, is consideration of merit (Cooper, 2011; Yancey, 2006). Advocates of colorblindness believe that race-conscious screening processes lead to lower-quality institutions because the hired/admitted minority applicants are often less qualified (Chan & Eyster, 2003). Faculty and staff attitudes toward the diversity initiative at GA generally reflected such an attitude. As Dr. Smith explained, one challenge he faced was the overarching faculty and staff attitude toward the initiative, which was along the lines of, "Just tell us what you want to do and tell us we're not going to sacrifice the integrity of our school." This attitude, I learned, is why GA administrators felt it was important that the school's diversity statement include a provision that the school's diversity efforts were not about setting targets for the numbers of diverse people it should hire or admit (GA Diversity Statement, 2013). And the administration's concerns were clearly warranted, as several faculty and staff shared with me their concerns about diversity targets/quotas. Specifically, they feared that in quantifying diversity goals and going to whatever lengths to achieve those, the school would have to compromise its Christian values, including its value in a colorblind meritocracy. The following two quotes illustrate such an attitude:

> I can tell you what it (diversity) doesn't mean for us. What it doesn't mean is what the secular press, the secular world calls diversity. They want equal this, equal that. It's almost entitlement in reverse. I don't know how to really explain that but it's almost *that*, and we can't have *that* in this school because we have certain. . . . It's again difficult because we have certain standards to have, and we will not compromise in a Christian setting, in a Christian organization. I don't know if you want to go into this, but you have different people groups. You have homosexuals, you have class, you have race, you have so many different things, but we can't compromise what the school was founded on and the biblical principles of why we exist. So, it's not just getting an equal amount of socioeconomic, spread the wealth around type thing; it's not that. It's not quotas, right?
> (Mr. Reed, a staff member)

> I think it (the initiative) means that Grace has a sincere interest in increasing diversity on this campus, which is good. I think it would be good to see more diversity here, but as Dr. Smith has repeatedly emphasized, not at the expense of Christian principles.
> (Mr. Vance, a teacher)

For GA faculty and staff, in particular, quantifying desired percentages of diverse students and staff seemed to mean that the school might have to hire or admit people that they believed did not represent and/or possess evangelical Christian values, like individuals identifying as LGBTQ, or as I will later discuss, certain types of black teachers and students.

Why Diversity Mattered

GA faculty and staff's belief in colorblindness was also reflected in their questioning of the school's motivations for developing the diversity initiative in the first place. In fact, it was in discussions of the school's reasons for addressing diversity that I saw the most variation among faculty and staff sensemaking about the initiative.

Some faculty and staff didn't view the diversity initiative as genuinely (meaning divinely) undertaken, but as one undertaken for strategic reasons. When I asked high school teacher, Mrs. Gallagher, for example, why she thinks the school created a diversity initiative, she responded,

To me, I think, blacks draw the line a lot. [. . .] I think it's become an issue again because society is making it an issue for us. I don't know that we really . . . I'm not sure why we need to address it either, absolutely. I mean, really. It's just kind of a given, I guess. We wanted to put it out there to make sure everybody understands that that's where we are. Make it more clear by putting it into words.

Emerson and Smith (2000) write that many white colorblind evangelicals blame racial minorities for exacerbating racial problems. And Mrs. Gallagher's statement reflects such a belief. She largely blamed the black community for making diversity an issue to which institutions have to respond. The subtext of her statement was the belief that doing something about diversity was a burden and merely a perfunctory gesture. Mrs. Gallagher went on to explain how adopting the initiative didn't require any real changes: "I don't think we really necessarily have changed." Adopting an approach to diversity that requires minimal accommodation is not surprising, as it is often multicultural initiatives "that take minimal effort to accommodate and do not force teachers to stray too far away from the standard curriculum, that are welcomed, and encouraged, in schools" (Jay, 2003, p. 6).

Other faculty and staff concurred that the diversity initiative only existed for strategic reasons. For example, Mrs. Dillard, another high school teacher, believed that the diversity initiative was simply a result of ACSI accreditation report: "I think it came from when we got ACSI certified and there was an indicator on it, and we fell short." Mrs. Dillard saw the school's diversity efforts as the result of a quasi-governmental intrusion, the kind of intrusion that many colorblind evangelicals blame for exacerbating racial problems (Emerson & Smith, 2000; Yancey, 2006).

Despite skepticism about the genuineness of GA's motivations for addressing diversity, some faculty and staff recognized spiritual reasons for caring about diversity in addition to strategic ones. For example, Mrs. Wheeler, a staff member stated, "Knowing that it came from the board of directors and the head of school, my hope is that, ultimately, God is the source of the inspiration, but I also think that we are living in a world where diversity is such a hot button issue that we need to respond to it." Likewise, Mr. Baxter, a high school teacher said, "I don't know if it's just for a political correctness position. I really believe that they have . . . I want to believe that they have enough sensitivity to recognize that the body of God, including our students, is diverse." And another teacher, Mr. Vance, explained,

> And you asked motivations, what I think is motivating them? I think mostly it's just a genuine love for the way God made the earth and a desire that we as a Christian school would not legitimately be ridiculed as racist.

These faculty and staff perceived that the administration's motivations were at least partly genuine.

Then some faculty and staff more fully embraced the biblical need to address diversity. Mr. Lang, a high school teacher, explained how because God is diverse via the Trinity, then the school should be diverse, adding that the current whiteness of the school "isn't biblical." And Mr. Gill, a middle school teacher, linked the school's need for diversity to its evangelical mission, stating, "I think it's a biblical mandate to be diverse and to reach out to all peoples, as we think Christian education is pretty much inseparable from evangelism." I wager that in any Christian school, the faculty and staff members who acknowledge "higher" reasons for diversity are more likely to buy into diversity efforts than those who only view the efforts as strategic. Viewing diversity efforts as the fulfillment of God's will for the school imbues the efforts with significance, especially in a community that renders commitment to Christ preeminent.

Also noteworthy was the variation among administrators' sensemaking about reasons to address diversity. Though all of the principals were involved in the creation of the school's diversity initiative, not all of the principals were as motivated by the ethical implications of not addressing it (i.e., the current demographics of the school are sending the wrong message to students) as was Dr. Smith. Principals Kline, Westerly, and Barnes, for example, believed that GA's primary motivation for addressing diversity concerned how the school appeared to the outside world. Principal Kline stated, "I think the purpose for a diversity statement is because the world expects you to have a diversity statement. I think that's why we have it." Principal Barnes similarly added,

> Diversity is a term co-opted by the secular world. It's their buzzword and in order to accommodate that to some extent because you're a Christian school in a predominantly secular world, you have to adopt this statement and do something about it.

Principal Westerly concurred and further explained that because colleges and universities were stressing diversity, GA felt pressure to respond:

> And it sounds, if you'll allow me, and I think this is part of the desire, we want kids who graduate from Duke. We want kids who graduate from MIT, Harvard, and Duke, and we want that.... There's a part of us that wants that and part of it I think comes out of a, part of it can be a pride thing, but part of it comes out of wanting the broader culture to understand that you can come to a Christian school like Grace, receive a Christ-oriented education, and still make it in medical school, that kind of thing.

According to Wagner (1997), Christian schools are open systems that "accommodat[e] to the surrounding American popular culture and the culture of the educational establishment," even as they try to avoid the "coercive isomorphism" that occurs from government regulation of schools (p. 20). And Principals Kline's and Westerly's statements confirmed that GA was not impervious to such normative and secular pressures.[12] Further, it is clear that GA's identity as perceived by secular institutions in its environment weighed on the administration's sensemaking about how to do diversity at GA. Dutton and Dukerich (1991) claim, "Individuals are personally motivated to preserve a positive organizational image and repair a negative one through association and disassociation with actions on issues" (as cited in Weick, 1995, p. 21). Principals Kline and Westerly recognized that the school's external image would be threatened if they did not "associate" with diversity in some capacity. Bracey and Moore (2017) claim that white institutions strategically seek only enough minorities "to defend against charges of racism" (p. 286), just as Hannah-Jones asserts that white schools seek only enough students of color (no more than 20%) to feel as though their kids are being exposed to diversity (as cited in Douglas, 2017).

But Principal Barnes recognized that choosing to address diversity in their own way might affect how the school is perceived. As he explained,

> I think our biggest challenge is philosophical, and it's not to get sucked into the diversity debate as it's defined by the secular culture. And I think that is going to bring the potential of not being identified or not being labeled as diverse at all.

Essentially, he realized that addressing diversity its own way may mean that the secular public does not recognize GA's diversity efforts as legitimate or enough.

Because some members of both the administration and the faculty and staff primarily believed that strategic reasons motivated GA to act on diversity, buy-in and genuine adoption of the initiative were difficult to obtain. Principal Kline, for instance, said to me, "You can probably tell by the tone of my voice, I get very frustrated about the issues of diversity because it's just not a big deal to me. It is just not." But buy-in is important because, "if the school community does not agree about the importance of diversity, everyone loses," and organizational leaders are central to communicating that importance (Young, Madsen, & Young et al., 2010, p. 139). In their study, Young et al. (2010) determine that motivations for addressing diversity matter in terms of if and how plans are implemented. For instance, they reported that principals refused to carry out a district's diversity initiative because the principals determined the district did not really value diversity, but rather established a diversity initiative only to satisfy public demands.[13]

Even though Dr. Smith was personally convinced of the importance of diversity, I observed that when he presented the school's diversity statement to faculty, he made the statement seem like a formality by emphasizing how crafting a diversity statement was the "top recommendation of ACSI" and how lawyers modified GA's statement to "keep the school out of any trouble" (observation, November 4, 2013). He also unintentionally trivialized diversity by using humor throughout the faculty meeting to ease tensions. For example, Dr. Smith pointed out the whiteness of the room as problematic, and then said, "If it wasn't for [a Hispanic teacher's name], we would be in big trouble," to which everyone laughed (observation, November 4, 2013). As they laughed, the Hispanic teacher got up and walked to the back of the room, presumably to get a drink, though it is also quite possible that the teacher felt uncomfortable for being singled out. Also, in an attempt to keep the mood light, Dr. Smith told a personal story about how he learned a valuable lesson from stereotyping a man based on his ethnicity. While it was clear Dr. Smith wanted to tell this story as a way of demonstrating that everyone, himself included, could stand to learn more about diversity and embrace it, that wasn't how it came across. Instead of really emphasizing the lesson he learned, he used a stereotypical name for the person he mistakenly stereotyped so that people both gasped and laughed at the story. The story clearly landed as a joke because another speaker in the faculty meeting referred to the story to get a laugh later in the faculty meeting.

Yet another way that Dr. Smith attempted to gain buy-in for the diversity initiative in this faculty meeting was that he explained that diversity was an issue at the school because it had recently lost a black family over a "misunderstanding" involving a comment made by a school leader that the family perceived as racist (observation, November 4, 2013). Dr. Smith's use of the term "misunderstanding" may or may not have been an accurate description of what happened, but he also didn't emphasize the seriousness of a school leader being accused of racism. He stated instead that he wanted the family back and left it there.

In this faculty meeting, Dr. Smith had the opportunity to stress the importance of addressing diversity and to tell faculty his personal convictions for caring about diversity—which I personally found very genuine and convincing—but he did not take it. Dr. Smith framed diversity in this initial faculty meeting as both a superficial formality and a laughable matter, even though he did not personally seem to believe it was only that. Dr. Smith also provided no opportunity for teachers to discuss the meaning of the school's diversity statement, ask questions about it, or determine what it meant for their practice, which was consistent with GA's emphasis on authority. Coburn (2005) explains how school leaders greatly influence the implementation of initiatives through creating opportunities for collaboration. In GA's case, teachers were not given an opportunity to think collaboratively about how they could carry out the school's diversity initiative. And to be fair, Dr. Smith recognized that he took the wrong approach to introducing the initiative, because after the meeting, he asked me not to write too many details about the personal story he told and said his wife had advised him not to tell it because it could be considered offensive.

Dr. Smith's actions in this faculty meeting, however, are likely not uncommon. Research suggests that school leaders often feel "uncomfortable when addressing diversity-related issues" (Young et al., 2010, p. 150). They are unable to talk about the benefits of diverse schools, even if they can attest to the need for diversity (Young et al., 2010). Throughout my many conversations with Dr. Smith, he emphasized his perception that diversity was a sensitive issue at GA. In the faculty meeting described earlier, Dr. Smith clearly downplayed the importance of diversity at GA and told a funny story about diversity in an effort to mitigate faculty and staff discomfort with diversity. His emphasis on ACSI's role in the initiative's creation also suggested that he wanted faculty and staff to believe he had no choice but to address diversity, even though Dr. Smith felt personally convicted to address it. In ascribing the initiative to ACSI, faculty and staff wouldn't blame him, the new guy from up North, for making diversity an issue at their school, for potentially seeking (from their perspective) to further decrease the selectivity of the school, or for the school's early failed attempts to address diversity, which I discuss later. As Dr. Smith said of his attempts to address diversity for the first time at the school, "For the younger guy from up North to come into that kind of environment, I had to be careful." Despite his carefulness, though, faculty associated the diversity initiative and, more broadly speaking, school transformation, with the arrival of Dr. Smith. As Principal Beatty put it, "GA is more about internal change now than we've ever been. I think we just stayed the same for a long time. Then Dr. Smith came."

Discussion

The conservative Christian ideology that defined GA's school culture greatly shaped the way administrators, faculty, and staff made sense of diversity. It was an ideology familiar to and embraced (as a condition for employment) by school faculty and staff. As administrators, faculty, and staff figured out what doing diversity looked like for their school, they agreed that cultivating unity in Christ should remain the school's most important goal. They believed that drawing special attention to differences would divide the body of Christ and that practicing colorblindness and rejecting quotas were two ways to avoid such division. Further, the school's conservative Christian ideology led to a construction of diversity that excluded certain groups of people, thereby shaping who the school would admit and hire.

As the following chapters reveal, GA's conservative Christian framing of diversity ended up having very real implications for its stakeholders, especially its students, parents, and teachers of color. GA's construction of diversity reinforced many of the school's existing practices, and in doing so undermined the steps the school was taking to become more diverse and create a climate that celebrated diversity. Moreover, the conflict between GA's construction of diversity and activities that would presumably enable it to meet its diversity goals (e.g., quantifying desired demographics and explicitly teaching about diversity) resulted in the school selectively employing quotas and color-attuned practices. And the goals of attaining an ethnically and socioeconomically diverse staff and student body and educating students about diverse others proved secondary to preserving the school's Christian identity as they defined it.

Notes

1 Blosser, 2017 also provides an abbreviated description of the school and its demographics.
2 All of the demographics reported in this chapter are from 2013/2014, the years in which I was collecting data. I point this out because today GA's student demographics are quite different, as one will see in the concluding chapter.
3 A pseudonym.
4 This percentage included faculty and staff children, who received a 40% discount on tuition.
5 A small city is defined as a city with a population between 100,000 and 250,000 (Kotkin, 2014).
6 I define ideology as a "shared, relatively coherently interrelated set of emotionally charged beliefs, values, and norms that bind some people together and help them to make sense of their worlds" (Trice and Beyer, 1993, p. 33; as cited in Weick, 1995, p. 111). GA's particular ideology had a theological base.
7 GA was already accredited by the Southern Association of Colleges and Schools, but the former head of school had decided to seek dual accreditation with ACSI.
8 I intentionally chose to describe the content of GA's diversity statement rather than directly quote it in order to protect the identity of my research site.
9 GA's diversity initiative is also briefly described in Blosser, 2017.
10 Staff member, Mrs. Bishop, told me that some teachers acknowledged Martin Luther King Jr. Day and cited an example, but I did not observe any activity or hear about such activities from any other participant.
11 For example, middle school teacher Mr. Gill asked, "What could be more biblical than to say that one day we'd have a race where people are judged by the content or a world where people are judged by the content of their character and not the color of their skin?" And even an administrator, Principal Westerly, said, "We have a means to bring unity to diversity so that we can largely, in our actions, do what Martin Luther King argued we should do. We should judge the character of the man not by his—we judge people by their character not by their skin color."
12 GA was open to influence from the educational establishment in other ways as well. For example, GA offered AP courses, even though faculty disagreed with and (as I discuss in a subsequent chapter) altered the AP curriculum to reflect conservative Christian ideology.
13 Young et al. (2010) is also described in Blosser, 2017.

References

Blosser, A. H. (2017). Considerations for addressing diversity in Christian Schools. In D. B. Hiatt-Michael (Ed.), *Family and community engagement in faith-based schools* (pp. 33–55). Charlotte, NC: Information Age Publishing, Inc.

Bracey, G. E., & Moore, W. L. (2017). "Race tests": Racial boundary maintenance in white evangelical churches. *Sociological Inquiry, 87*(2), 282–302.

Chan, J., & Eyster, E. (2003). Does banning affirmative action lower college student quality. *The American Economic Review, 93*(3), 858–872.

Chou, D., & others. (1982). Discriminatory religious schools and tax exempt status. *Commission on Civil Rights.* Retrieved from https://files.eric.ed.gov/fulltext/ED228712.pdf

Coburn, C. E. (2005). Shaping teacher sensemaking: School leaders and the enactment of reading policy. *Educational Policy, 19*(3), 476–509.

Cooper, R. (2011). Enhancing the schooling experience of African American students in predominantly white independent schools: Conceptual and strategic considerations to developing a critical third space. In D. T. Slaughter-Defoe, H. C. Stevenson, E. G. Arrington, & D. J. Johnson (Eds.), *Black educational choice: Assessing the private and public alternatives to traditional K–12 public schools* (pp. 222–233). Santa Barbara, CA: ABC-CLIO, LLC.

Douglas, D. (2017, December 14). Are private schools immoral: A conversation with Nikole Hannah-Jones about race, education, and democracy. *The Atlantic.* Retrieved from www.theatlantic.com/education/archive/2017/12/progressives-are-undermining-public-schools/548084/

Dutton, J. E., & Dukerich, J. M. (1991). Keeping an eye on the mirror: Image and identity in organizational adaption. *Academy of Management Journal, 34,* 517–554.

Emerson, M. O., & Smith, C. (2000). *Divided by faith: Evangelical religion and the problem of race in America.* New York, NY: Oxford UP.

Flowers, R. B. (2005). *That godless court?* (2nd ed.). Louisville, KY: Westminster John Knox Press.

Gutmann, A. (1987). *Democratic education.* Princeton, NJ: Princeton UP.

Harris, D. M. (2012). Diversity in the Christian school. In T. P. Wiens & K. L. Wiens (Eds.), *Building a better school: Essays on exemplary Christian school leadership* (pp. 197–211). Stoney Brook, NY: Paideia Press.

Jay, M. (2003). Critical race theory, multicultural education, and the hidden curriculum of hegemony. *Multicultural Perspectives, 5*(4), 3–9.

Kotkin, J. (2014, September 3). America's fastest-growing small cities. *Forbes.* Retrieved from www.forbes.com/fdc/welcome_mjx.shtml

Nevin, D., & Bills, R. E. (1976). *The schools that fear built: Segregationist academies in the South.* Washington, DC: Acropolis Books Ltd.

Parsons, P. F. (1987). *Inside America's Christian schools.* Macon, GA: Mercer University Press.

Peshkin, A. (1986). *God's choice: The total world of a fundamentalist Christian school.* Chicago, IL: University of Chicago Press.

Rose, S. (1988). *Keeping them out of the hands of Satan: Evangelical schooling in America.* New York, NY: Routledge, Chapman and Hall, Inc.

Rose, S. (1993). Christian fundamentalism and education in the United States. In M. Marty & R. S. Appleby (Eds.), *Fundamentalisms and society* (pp. 452–489). Chicago, IL: University of Chicago Press.

Trice, H. M., & Beyer, J. M. (1993). *The cultures of work organizations.* Englewood Cliffs, NJ: Prentice Hall.

Wagner, M. B. (1990). *God's schools: Choice and compromise in American society.* New Brunswick, NJ: Rutgers University Press.

Wagner, M. B. (1997). Generic conservative Christianity: The demise of denominationalism in Christian schools. *Journal for the Scientific Study of Religion, 36*(1), 13–24.

Weick, K. E. (1995). *Sensemaking in organizations.* Thousand Oaks, CA: Sage Publications.

Yancey, G. (2006). *Beyond racial gridlock: Embracing mutual responsibility.* Downers Grove, IL: InterVarsity Press.

Young, B. L., Madsen, J., & Young, M. A. (2010). Implementing diversity plans: Principals' perception of their ability to address diversity in their schools. *NASSP Bulletin, 94*(2), 135–157.

Note: I exclude references that might in any way compromise the identity of the school.

3 Prioritizing Fit
Grace Academy's Recruitment and Retention Practices

One overarching goal of GA's diversity initiative was the recruitment of a racially, ethnically, and socioeconomically diverse faculty, staff, and student body (GA Diversity Statement, 2013).[1] This chapter analyzes the sensemaking of GA's administrators as they sought to implement that goal. I focus on administrators' sensemaking specifically because they were the people primarily responsible for figuring out how to achieve GA's diversity goals. In trying to achieve unity in Christ, GA's administration practiced a model of student and faculty recruitment based on "fit." Numerous factors shaped their sensemaking: conservative Christian ideology, organizational identity, school norms, experiences of neighboring Christian schools, school leaders' racial identities and attitudes, and stances of GA parents and donors. GA experienced many challenges in implementing its recruitment and retention goals because of the prevailing racial, political, and gender norms at the school.

I use some of the tenets of Critical Race Theory (CRT) to guide my analysis of GA's recruitment and retention practices. CRT maintains that when minorities fail or refuse to uphold the prevailing norms of the dominant group in institutions (like schools), such actions can result in their exclusion or marginalization. The theory also problematizes attitudes, policies, and practices that emphasize racial neutrality, such as colorblindness (Esposito, 2011; Evans, 2007). CRT enriches an understanding of how GA's practices specifically affected students and teachers of color, since these were the primary populations GA was trying to recruit and retain. Therefore, I consider the ways in which GA privileged certain norms and values over others and the impact of those norms on students and teachers across racial differences. I also critically examine the notions of meritocracy and colorblindness that guided GA's recruitment processes and daily practices.

About 9% of GA's students identified as students of color, which was and still is well below the 30% national average for conservative Christian schools (NCES, 2017). GA's percentage had remained relatively static over the prior three years. A majority of GA's students of color identified as African American. Similarly, of Grace Academy's 116 faculty and staff members, only 5 were persons of color (4%), which is also well below national averages for independent schools.[2] That said, GA took many significant steps to become more diverse, including hiring a diversity coordinator, advertising available positions on an employment website for ethnic minorities, featuring students of color in advertising materials, and offering scholarships to members of local black churches.[3]

The Recruitment and Retention of Students of Color

In conversations about student recruitment, I repeatedly heard from GA administrators that it was important that minority students were good "fits" for the school. Considering "fit" was the administration's alternative to setting targets for their desired percentages of minority students. To illustrate, Principal Kline explained his thought process when deciding which students to admit:

> When I'm looking at an applicant, I don't even pay attention to whether they're black or white or Hispanic or Indian or Asian. Never crosses my . . . I mean eventually I realize that (the applicant's race), but I never go into it that way. And here's what happens: if I read and look in this and I begin to look down here, and I see these students and I think, "Oh, well that's a person of a different ethnic background than white. Well that's good." But I don't say, "Oh if I've got a white child, and I've got an Asian child, I'm going to choose the Asian child because I've got to have ten of those." It's who fits and what we can do for them and what they can do for us. And when I say what they can do for us, I don't mean oh they can play football, or they can sing or blow a horn. . . . It's just, "is it a fit?"

Principal Kline and the administration's sensemaking about recruitment was shaped by the school community's belief in colorblindness because their plan involved recruiting a diverse student body without intentionally considering students' races. Further, the administration's approach reflected a belief in meritocracy that is common among advocates of colorblindness (Yancey, 2006). They primarily considered what students could add to the school in terms of their talents, and, ultimately, they wanted who best "fit." This idea of fit, however, must be unpacked. The administration's emphasis on "fit" meant that students of color, and more specifically black students, were held more rigorously to the school's conservative Christian ideals, yet the black students who were deemed to "fit" claimed to have positive schooling experiences.

Unpacking Fit

During my time at GA, I learned that "fit" meant something different for black student applicants than it did for white student applicants, even though some members of the administration didn't explicitly admit or even recognize it. I did not hear if notions of "fit" differed for students from backgrounds other than black and white because when GA stakeholders discussed recruitment and retention practices for "diverse" students, they usually were referring to black students and teachers. GA administrators were interested in admitting black students from two-parent homes, from families who desired a Christian education, and "good kids" who would assimilate to GA's culture rather than try to change it. One administrator explained GA's process of selection for the black football players they admitted:

> I know everyone wants to come. You pick the most. . . . The kids who are most qualified, who meet our mission . . . so these are good kids who integrate like that (snaps fingers) because they're coming from good families; these are good kids. They're just families who want a Christian school, so we can be very, very, highly selective because so many are trying to come down. So there's another school somewhere in this community who isn't. They have a football program, so they're bringing in a lot of kids. The things that we hear . . . I have to be very careful here. The things we hear is, 'Okay, you bring in 20 kids in high school, and they're not all coming from a two-parent household or they're not coming . . . they're there to play football, hopefully get a scholarship for college.' It could have an opposite effect and it is . . . because they'll come over and say, 'We don't like how this is changing the culture of the school.' The kids that we bring in, our culture goes to them, so they don't create their own subculture.

The experiences of neighboring schools are seen here to be part of the context that shaped the administration's sensemaking about student recruitment. They wanted a diverse student body but did not want diverse students who were going to alter the culture of the school or create division between the black and white students, as had purportedly happened at a nearby school. So this administrator claimed that GA was selective about the minority students it admitted. GA administrators only admitted students they believed would easily assimilate to GA's culture. GA is not alone in this practice. Other studies of predominantly white schools reveal that black students are welcome when they "fit in" (Hatt-Echeverria & Jo, 2005, p. 61).

There did not seem to be the same emphasis on fit for the white students GA accepted. Coming from a two-parent home mattered more for black students trying to attend GA, and the administration boasted that most of the black students GA admitted came from such families. The implicit bias was that black students from two-parent homes were going to be better behaved (i.e., "good kids") and more likely to fit. But white families were not held to the same standard. In fact, faculty and staff explained just how prevalent divorced families were at GA, making comments like, "I think that we have a lot more families that are divorced, ugly divorces that we would never have seen years ago" (Mrs. Dillard, a teacher), and "there is much more divorce [now] than there was when I came here" (Principal Kline). Yet this reality in African American families appeared to be undesirable.[4] As an example of GA's apparent different admissions standards, I interviewed a white student who was recruited to GA from another country, specifically for athletics. I learned that he came from a divorced family and had a history of alcohol, drug use, and fighting, all facts he openly shared with his classmates and faculty. These characteristics were not what typically defined a "good kid" at GA, yet they did not inhibit this student's admission nor the determination that he would fit GA's culture.

Yet high standards of selectivity for nonwhite students were not universally deemed to be a bad thing. Mrs. Poole, a black parent at GA, wished the school would hold all students to the high standards of selectivity that students of color had to meet:

> If there are some students that are coming in there, black, Latino, whoever, and they're in a gang? [. . .] I mean, if they're coming in and they going to bring something that's not going to be positive, we don't want you in there whatever color you . . . you know?

From her perspective, then, all of the students GA admits should be "good" kids.

The Importance of Christian Faith

Key among the characteristics needed to fit in at GA was adherence to a Christian faith. Though GA's conservative Christian beliefs and values may have limited which students fit at the school, the black students who held Christian beliefs and were deemed to fit by the administration did have their schooling experiences strengthened by their shared faith. GA wanted black students who were Christian, as demonstrated by the financial incentives they offered to families who were members of local black churches.[5] Also, all student applicants, regardless of race, had to have a pastor's recommendation and write an essay about their relationship with Jesus Christ as part of their application for admission.[6] Consistent with other research on black students at white schools (e.g., Herndon & Hirt, 2004; Hughes, 1987; Kraft, 1991), I found that Christian faith was an important resource for African American students as they processed their schooling experiences at GA, particularly those experiences related to race. John and Elijah, both African American students, provided two of the most powerful examples. John explained how his Christian faith helped him not to focus on his minority status at GA and instead—in keeping with GA's emphasis on Christian unity—to see him and his classmates as "one":

> It (his faith in God) teaches me . . . live your day to the fullest of your ability. Who cares if you're the only black kid in school? Who cares if you are the only black on the . . . team?[7] It's just . . . we're all one. God looks at us as one. Live through Him, and He will do the rest.

Similarly to John, Elijah's faith guided him to focus on his classmates' personalities, not their races—a reflection of the colorblindness GA taught. He also recognized his and his classmates' common goals:

> We (GA students) don't really see race; that may come from the biblical perspective . . . we don't . . . in the Bible, not many races are called out. [. . .] We tend to follow that. We call people by their names and how they make us feel . . . your personality describes you, not your race. Whether they're minority, African American, whatever . . . everybody has the same mind-set, to be successful and be a Christian. We don't really look at race; race is not even an issue. Me coming here, a lot of people asked how I felt being around a lot of different people outside of my race, and I said I didn't think about it. I see people as individuals, not as color.

Thus, John and Elijah indicated that their Christian faith helped them to experience the very thing GA desired for its students: unity in Christ. Elijah went on to tell me that he also valued being able to pray about his problems with his classmates, noting, "You always have an escape route for your problem . . . and that is religion." Similarly, Denise, another African American student, discussed how the Christian context of the school generally made a difference in the way minority students were treated:

> For the most part, we are definitely a lot nicer to each other than I guess the public school would be. Because in public school, when I went a long time ago, they tell us the Golden Rule, "Do unto others as you would have them do unto you." And here we can talk about it a lot more and how it has to do with God and stuff like that. How He said you have to be nice towards everybody, no matter what their skin color is or where they're from. Stuff like that. [. . .] There's always just like either in the back of your mind or in the front of your mind, you need to be nice to everybody because that's what the Bible says.

Denise maintained that the Golden Rule meant more at a Christian school because students viewed it as a biblical mandate. John made a similar statement in saying that it was his classmates' Christian perspective that prevented racial discrimination at the school:

Me: What does it mean to think about diversity or difference from a biblical or Christian perspective in your mind?

John: Well . . . Christian perspective . . . Here, people, they don't discriminate against your color. They look at you as one, as you're like a brother; you're like blood. From a Christian standpoint, it's not about what's on the outside that matters. It's what's on the inside that counts.

Within the conservative Christian ideology, these students' perspectives suggest that Christian schools may be more conducive environments to Christian minority students than other types of schools and that restricting the admission of minority students to those who identify as Christians may be beneficial to both the school and students. A CRT analysis of these comments, though, might see an oppressor consciousness at work, making students of color submissive to the dominant colorblind ideology that privileges whiteness as normative.

When it came to meeting the student recruitment goals of the diversity initiative, GA administrators determined that "fit" for newly admitted students was more important than just increasing the number of racial/ethnic minority students. Characteristics like family composition and Christian faith appeared to matter more for racial/ethnic minority students than they did for white students because such characteristics helped the administration identify "good" minority kids. By treating fit differently for black students, GA was using race as a specific factor in their decision making, which violated their attested belief in colorblindness. Yet true unity in Christ, at least as it was perceived by GA, can't lead to differentiated admissions standards. On the other hand, admitting students based on fit could under the right circumstances promote GA's second goal of creating a culture that celebrates diversity as unity in Christ, because if they didn't admit based on fit, then they might undercut their unity, as evidenced by the divisive subcultures that reportedly sprung up at the neighboring school.

The Recruitment and Retention of Teachers of Color

GA's diversity initiative also called for more faculty of color. Administrators recognized that hiring diverse teachers would help them recruit more diverse students and cultivate the climate they desired. With a goal to hire more teachers of color, GA administrators had to figure out if and how they should change their hiring practices. I discovered that administrators' sensemaking reinforced the school's existing practice of recruiting and maintaining a predominantly white teaching faculty because the school prioritized "fit" within its white, conservative Christian framework.

As with students, GA's emphasis on fit led to a tension in hiring and retaining minority faculty: the school espoused both a desire to be more diverse and to remain colorblind. Even as GA advertised positions on an employment site for people of color, the administration wanted to minimize the importance of race in the hiring process, a notion consistent with colorblindness. Principal Kline explained his approach to hiring:

> It is absolutely important to me when I am looking and interviewing a person, I look at, there are two things I look at. [. . .] And one is that they are academically sound in who they are as an educator to be able to teach these children, because academically, we are an academic institution. And that is of utmost importance, so that's what I look at. And the second thing that I look at is their . . . their spiritual life and who they are. There are those that have been Christian for a long, long time and are very settled in their personal relationship with Jesus. It's more important to me that you have a personal relationship. [. . .] It doesn't matter if you go to church or—well obviously you're going to go to church—but it doesn't matter to me what church you attend. That's not it. It's a personal relationship. So those are the two things that I look at. We have had, we've had teachers of . . . you know different races that come here and interview. Most of the teachers that we have here on the. . .[8] staff are just white Americans. It has nothing to do with the fact that I'm interested in hiring all white people.

Principal Kline reported that he gives little weight to applicants' races in the hiring process, but he gives applicants' religious beliefs great weight. As with many other Christian schools, religious beliefs were so important in hiring decisions at GA that teacher contracts included a statement wherein teachers had to affirm that they were "born-again" Christians and agree to be Christian role models to students (GA Employment Contract, 2013).

The school's emphasis on fit, though, also led to a different standard for minority faculty: they had to demonstrate a higher level of fit with institutional norms than other faculty, suggesting the administration was not as colorblind as it professed. While Christian faith was one of the two most important qualifications for hiring teachers (according to Principal Kline), in practice, there appeared to be additional desired qualifications for black teachers. Like with black student admissions, black teachers' ability to fit the norms of the school mattered not only for hiring but also for retention. The experience of GA's first black teacher, Mrs. Griffin, demonstrates the contextual factors that shaped the administration's sensemaking about faculty recruitment. Her case brings home the fundamental tension between seeking diversity while prioritizing a particular concept of Christian colorblindness.

A Legitimizing Myth

I heard the story of Mrs. Griffin on my first visit to GA, when I was trying to determine whether or not the school would be a good place to pursue my research.[9] She was GA's first black teacher of an academic subject,[10] whom they had hired in a previous year. Dr. Smith, the school's headmaster, told me that diversity would be a sensitive issue to discuss in GA's community because of the situation with Mrs. Griffin. When I raised my eyebrows at this comment, Dr. Smith proceeded to tell me that he had to dismiss Mrs. Griffin after only one year at GA, but that her dismissal was not about her race.

Before I tell Mrs. Griffin's story, I need to note that I am telling her story as relayed to me by numerous people in the school. As a researcher, I recognize that Mrs. Griffin's side of the story would add an important perspective, and I believe in giving voice to marginalized people. I can say with certainty, however, that asking for her contact information or reaching out to her would have destroyed the trust it took me so long to cultivate with school stakeholders. Because of the circumstances under which she was dismissed and the defensive postures of some stakeholders when we discussed her, I am positive that school stakeholders would have assumed I was out to accuse them of racism, which was not my intention or goal. And after the hoops I had to jump through just to get into the school, I was not about to risk losing their trust or access. Instead, I analyze school stakeholders' sensemaking about the situation with Mrs. Griffin, which reveals a lot about the organizational norms and ideology that shaped GA's approach to diversity.

Mrs. Griffin was hired to teach middle school. Dr. Smith was initially very proud of his hire, as it was progress toward the school's goal to hire more minority faculty. As he explained, "In a pool of applications, this African American had her master's degree, had very strong recommendations from a public school. We thought it was a slam dunk; we got a professional. This is good. We got a great start." Dr. Smith's comment suggests that African American applicants' professional backgrounds mattered tremendously—they had to be perceived as qualified. Being perceived as qualified is especially important for teachers of color entering a community like GA's that questions whether diversity enhancement programs, like Affirmative Action, are able to ensure equally qualified minority candidates. Despite Mrs. Griffin's qualifications, her performance did not meet the administration's expectations, and they decided not to renew her contract for a second year. Administrators repeatedly told me that her dismissal was not a racial issue and emphasized that they ended on good terms with Mrs. Griffin. Principal Barnes, for instance, said in justification of her dismissal, "It was truly technical. Just pieces within the instruction that were deficient." When I pressed him a bit more, he explained that her deficiency was in the "content" area. But race appeared to, at the very least, factor into Mrs. Griffin's dismissal in ways that the administration perhaps couldn't recognize or subconsciously didn't want to recognize from within their white, conservative Christian, colorblind perspective.

Anderson's (1990) concept of "legitimizing myths" is useful in analyzing the administration's explanations of Mrs. Griffin's dismissal (as cited in Evans, 2007, p. 162). Legitimizing myths are part of sensemaking in that they help people resolve "ideological contradictions" (Evans, 2007, p. 162). By insisting that Mrs. Griffin's dismissal was not about race, school administrators could resolve the tension they likely felt between their stated desire in the diversity initiative to have a more diverse faculty and the apparently stronger desire for that diversity to fit within their preexisting framework of Christian unity. Evans (2007) notes that these myths "inevitably serve to legitimate existing social structures" (p. 162). In this case, the myth legitimated the school's colorblind approach, its emphasis on fit as a qualification for "good" diversity, and the widely held belief that race is an individual, not systemic, reality. From the administration's perspective, Mrs. Griffin was released because of her own actions and inability to teach the course's content, not because of larger systemic issues endemic to the school.

Not everyone at the school, however, believed in the particular legitimizing myth that Mrs. Griffin's dismissal was not about race. Principal Barnes suspected that Mrs. Griffin saw things a bit differently:

> And if you were to ask her, . . . I think she would say to you and in fact, I know she would because she shared this with me . . . that she felt that there was a part of this (her dismissal) that was because she was black.

White evangelical advocates of colorblindness, like many GA stakeholders, often accuse people of color for making situations about race even if they are not (from the perspective of the white evangelicals) (Emerson & Smith, 2000). If Mrs. Griffin indeed felt that part of her dismissal was because she was black, then she was not alone. Mr. Howe, a white teacher, said, "I don't know all the specifics of the teacher last year leaving, but I know she had an incredibly rough year last year . . . I think a lot of the problems were brought on because she was black." Likewise, a white staff member, Mrs. Bishop, initially claimed that Mrs. Griffin was fired for having a "significantly different worldly outlook." But then she elaborated that the worldly outlook to which she was referring was rooted in cultural differences: "There are some cultural differences there, and right now, that can be a pretty dramatic difference." Even though Dr. Smith insisted and believed Mrs. Griffin was not ultimately let go because of her race, he knew many of the white parents' complaints about her were rooted in race, and he recognized that race played a large enough role in the situation that he felt it was necessary to bring in the black minister from Mrs. Griffin's church to mediate the conversations he had with her about her performance. He wanted the minister to help facilitate their negotiations in a Christian manner and ease any racial tensions that might arise in the conversations. Granted, the school had employment contracts that mandated private, Christian negotiation to settle disputes,[11] but Dr. Smith's approach, at the very least, shows he suspected Mrs. Griffin might see the circumstances influencing her dismissal to be affected by her race. And Principal Barnes too acknowledged the possibility that Mrs. Griffin's race may have played a part in why she wasn't "well received" by the GA community and explained how he couldn't assure me there were no biases or prejudices at GA. Teacher Mr. Howe explained that he believed Mrs. Griffin wanted to stay at GA, but added that "if you're beaten down all the time, and you have parents questioning you all the time, I mean that will just wear a person out."

Though many at the school believed that race was not involved in Mrs. Griffin's dismissal, even those people who recognized the role of race tended to see racism as an individual reality. That is, the prevailing belief in the school was that individuals, not structures, are responsible for social problems, such as racism and poverty. Emerson and Smith (2000) observe that because white evangelicals believe so strongly in the power of sin as an individual reality, they tend to view such problems to be the results of individual sin. Hatt-Echeverria and Jo (2005) locate such an attitude more broadly in middle- and upper-class white communities. They (2005) argue that because many whites view racism as an action carried out by individuals, they can "adopt a pseudo-liberal rhetoric of promoting diversity without pushing for the change of institutional or structural issues then define themselves as 'innocent' and absolved of their participation in reproducing racial inequities" (p. 52). Leaders operating with this mind-set can blame individuals for attributing problems to their race instead of examining how institutional policies, practices, and biases may have caused or contributed to the problem (Hatt-Echeverria & Jo, 2005). This appeared to describe the case with Mrs. Griffin because some members of GA's administration criticized her for her failure as a teacher instead of acknowledging the racism and institutional norms of whiteness that made it more difficult for her to do her job.

Deep-rooted beliefs in colorblindness enable communities to overlook racialized norms. As Lewis (2001) writes,

> Rather than a benign phenomenon, in many ways [colorblindness] helps to enable all members of [a] community to avoid confronting the racial realities that surround them, to avoid facing their own racist presumptions and understandings, and to avoid dealing with racist events (by deracializing them). Moreover, it does this as it enables

people to feel as if they are on righteous terrain by following in the footsteps of Martin Luther King Jr.

(p. 801)

So when one couples a belief in individual sin with an ethos of colorblindness, it is no wonder that the narrative concerning Mrs. Griffin was what it was. A deeper look into Mrs. Griffin's case, however, reveals the larger structures of race, gender, and politics that factored into the kind of minority faculty member GA expected.

Politics, Femininity, and Race

Numerous participants reported that Mrs. Griffin's difficulties at GA began almost immediately upon her hire. On the first day of teacher in-service training, prior to the start of school, Mrs. Griffin wore a shirt promoting President Obama. In doing so, she violated GA's conservative political norms and the school's expectations of appropriate feminine dress and passivity. Wearing this shirt set Mrs. Griffin up for a difficult year. Mr. Armstrong, a teacher, said in his interview with me, "Mrs. Griffin . . . she couldn't adapt. She couldn't adapt. She couldn't adapt. I mean she was fired on the first day. She came in here with an Obama shirt on." Later in the interview, Mr. Armstrong reemphasized, "The reason why she got fired was because she wore an Obama shirt. I ain't lying. Bottom line. It don't matter if she has a genius mind. It wouldn't have mattered." Several other faculty and staff also mentioned the Obama shirt to me as an example of her poor choices. Dr. Smith and I had the following conversation about it:

Dr. Smith: I had to be very careful. I think this is such a conservative traditional environment, no one ever came in here and challenged me on that, but I know there's plenty of chitchat about it, about, 'Wow, now we're hiring a [diversity] coordinator. That means you're going to hire people that perhaps . . . hire people who aren't as qualified.' And that was the perception I gave when we hired that woman who showed up on day one, the first day of in-service, which everybody had come to, with the big . . .
Me: The big Obama shirt? I heard about the Obama shirt. Like I said . . .
Dr. Smith: She could have been my partner; you know what I mean? She had a wonderful opportunity to impact 1,300 families and threw it away. That's too bad. That's how I view that.

Dr. Smith's comment indicates the presence of a common societal belief at GA: that increasing diversity within an organization means a reduction in quality (Chan & Eyster, 2003). With schools in particular, people commonly express concern that the blacker a school becomes, the lower the standards of the school (Brown, 2011; Scott, 2005). Further, Dr. Smith maintained that Mrs. Griffin's choice to wear an Obama shirt made it so that she was perceived as less qualified, which suggests that the GA staff's most valued qualification for black teachers was not academic credentials, but rather fit. In this case, she didn't fit because of her defiance (whether intentional or not) of the school's prevailing conservative political stance and its standards of femininity. But instead of finding fault with such community perceptions, some GA faculty and staff blamed Mrs. Griffin for selecting clothing that created those perceptions.

The conservative politics of the school were palpable. While I was there, the school hosted a conservative politician who was promoting a school voucher program. They also hosted an event in which a Tea Party 2016 presidential hopeful came to speak to students. In addition, Dr. Smith sometimes wrote blogs to encourage families to vote with conservatives on certain issues. And most students were politically conservative as well. Some students even reportedly covered another student's car with "Nobama" stickers when he revealed his left-leaning political views.

Conservative Christian norms of female passivity and submission were also evident at GA. Male and female students were separated during physical education (PE) classes, and male students learned in PE to recite a creed about becoming strong men. Likewise, some students reported learning in Bible classes that men were the heads of household and that women should be obedient to them. And I observed that women were rarely invited to speak in chapel or serve as student chaplains. Moreover, I noticed that during morning meetings in the gym, female teachers sat together in the front of the bleachers with the students, while the male teachers stood together against the wall facing the students, able to observe students' behavior. The same was often true for chapel services, where male teachers stood in the back of the room or sat in the back row. These postures conveyed that male teachers were the disciplinarians and guardians. Female teachers also ate at a separate lunch table than the male teachers. And both male and female teachers were expected to dress modestly and nicely. Only on field trips or during special events did I see teachers wearing T-shirts, and these were always GA shirts. Mrs. Griffin's Obama T-shirt defied the school's norms of feminine passivity and modesty both in its casualness and its content. It communicated that she was a woman who had an opinion that she wanted to make known.

Mrs. Griffin's willingness to express her opinion continued into the school year, upsetting parents. While volunteering at the school, one highly involved white parent reported to Dr. Smith that she overheard Mrs. Griffin speaking loudly and angrily to her students, apparently upsetting and intimidating them. Other parents heard of the situation and called for Mrs. Griffin's immediate termination, though Dr. Smith and the administration kept her through the end of the year. It is possible that Mrs. Griffin was acting inappropriately in her interactions with students, but it also may be that parents regarded her style of authority as incompatible with the school's norms of female passivity and white femininity. Perhaps parents reacted more harshly to her loudness because she was black, which has happened in other white school communities (e.g., Holland, 2012; Ispa-Landa, 2013; Morris, 2006).

Culturally Relevant Pedagogy vs. Colorblindness

Mrs. Griffin also shunned GA's norm of colorblindness and employed what scholars identify as culturally relevant pedagogy (CRP). That is, Mrs. Griffin reportedly gave assignments that included the voices of people from various cultural backgrounds in an effort to build cultural competence. She also gave assignments designed to raise students' critical consciousness about societal and historical inequities (Ladson-Billings, 1995). Parents and some members of the administration deemed her practice of CRP as her "agenda," which did not fit the school's culture of a pedagogy that promoted Christian unity. Principal Barnes described Mrs. Griffin's approach:

> But there was a sense of a, you know I think there was a little bit of an agenda. Um, and I don't think that's wrong necessarily; it comes out of the background of who we are. We all have an agenda that comes out of our background. I don't know that our student body was . . . I don't know if it's that they weren't ready for it. I think there were some other factors that caused some of that to not be well received. Um, I know one unit, one book report, she required that it be a book written by a minority author. Well, I don't think that's a bad thing to do. But it wasn't well received, and it wasn't well received I don't think because of that piece (minority authorship), as much as because there were some other things that had happened . . . that she kind of put herself in a position at that point that I'm not sure anything was going to be well received.

Dr. Smith described another assignment Mrs. Griffin gave:

> She brought in a picture of a black plow woman and had the kids write an assignment, which was totally appropriate. Some parent did some research and that picture came from [an article titled] "An Angry, Pissed-Off N—[12]" or something like that. It was a website of some sort of the oppression; it was the oppression of the white man against the black people. It was that offensive! So that photo went with that article, and she brought that in our class. "Whoa! What do I do with that one?" I can't remember if I brought that up

to her but at that point—this was towards the end of the year—we already knew (that GA was going to let her go), we were going to lose a whole lot of families (if GA didn't let her go), and we were really sacrificing the integrity of our program because she wasn't very strong. She did come around and survive the rest of the year, but when you're dealt with that, that . . . this picture and here's the title of it . . . she just removed the title.

From these descriptions, it seems that Mrs. Griffin wanted students to recognize the contributions of minority writers and think critically about white people's historic oppression of African Americans. Notably, these goals were not deemed inappropriate by the administration. But these goals were also not in keeping with the school's norm of colorblind ideology or their theological belief in unity. A teaching agenda that emerged from a white, politically conservative, colorblind perspective would likely have been accepted. While Principal Barnes reasoned that the parent disapproval of the minority author assignment might not have been exclusively about Mrs. Griffin's race or agenda, Dr. Smith admitted that parent disapproval of another assignment was connected to race and their discomfort with the idea of being depicted as white oppressors. After all, acknowledging oppression does not promote unity. The administration was faced with the decision of whether to keep Mrs. Griffin and potentially lose tuition-paying families or dismiss her. Ultimately, the administration sided with the parents and the school's norms.

According to one teacher, though, the administration's discomfort with CRP seemed to extend beyond Mrs. Griffin's use of it. In a conversation I had with a teacher, who asked for assurance of anonymity, I learned that while this teacher desired to teach works from different cultures, the teacher chose not to do so for fear of losing his job. The teacher explained that an administrator once reprimanded him for sharing his personal and somewhat socially progressive views on race with students, so he feared teaching anything that acknowledged cultural differences.

Other predominantly white school communities have also resisted CRP (e.g., Lewis, 2001; Mabokela & Madsen, 2003). The white, suburban schools that Mabokela and Madsen (2003) studied did not support black teachers' use of CRP and opted for colorblind curricula instead. Similarly, the predominantly white school Lewis (2001) studied didn't believe multicultural curricula was relevant to their school because of its mostly white student population. And a school board in Colorado resisted the new AP US History curriculum because it included an increased emphasis on women's rights, slavery, and other acts of civil disobedience and/or oppression (Slevin, 2014). CRP was seen to undermine GA's espoused view of Christian unity, which rested on the perceived biblical colorblindness of Colossians: "Here there is no Gentile or Jew."

Black Parents' Views on Teachers of Color

Though frustrated by Mrs. Griffin's experience at GA, black parents continued to desire teachers and/or administrators of color. These are the types of comments I heard from them:

> Let me see a credentialed black instructor. Not just a coach, a black instructor, teaching a meaningful course.
> (Mr. Curtis)

> Get some diversity in the front office. Get some diversity in somewhere other than the janitor and the cleaning lady.
> (Mr. Baldwin)

But black parents recognized that there were some barriers to securing black teachers at GA. One barrier they identified was white parents. Mr. Baldwin, a parent who interacted with Mrs. Griffin outside of school, said, "From what I heard, the parents gave her hell." The Poole family made a similar assertion. Black parents also identified GA's conservative political ethos as a potential barrier to the school becoming more diverse because such an ethos can cause many African Americans great discomfort. Four of the African American families I spoke with explained how disappointed they were with the rhetoric that circulated during the 2008 and 2012 elections. Mr. and Mrs. Jenkins described those elections as "the most tense time" at GA and complained that faculty and staff were readily making comments that reflected their conservative political leanings. The Pooles told me a similar story in my interview with them:

> Even Tommy (their son) felt the pressure with Obama. In school, it was real strong about that they were Republicans and talked against him, the teachers . . . some of the teachers. One of them, and I love them dearly . . . but she just said, "I am a George Bush fan." Even at work, we cannot just openly . . . we're not supposed to be going around saying. . . . Well, they did! She said we could go vote for him!
> (Mrs. Poole)

The Curtis's, another black family, expressed their frustration with teachers who shared their political views with students:

> You can't say, "This is what God says about that," when you're just trying to use an ultra-conservative view! God is not always ultra-conservative. Jesus was . . . in some things, when he returned to save people, he was extremely liberal.
> (Mr. Curtis)

The conservative politics of the school alienated many black families. Though black churches are often theologically conservative—like GA and the white evangelical tradition from which it comes—black churches tend to lean left politically (Mellowes, 2010). In fact, 69% of black evangelicals identify as Democrats (Bacon Jr. & Thomson-DeVeaux, 2018), and black voters supported Barack Obama, a democrat, at a rate of around 84% (Newport, 2014). Black parents at GA liked the conservative theology that the school taught, but they disagreed that such theology naturally leads to the prevailing conservative politics of the school.

Given these realities, black parents acknowledged that only a certain kind of black person would be a successful teacher at GA. I had the following conversation with Mrs. Poole:

Mrs. Poole: That experience they had with that African American teacher last year, to me, clearly showed that (white parents) was the reason. It was the parents, and the reasons why I can't leave. The parents are not quite ready for that, and there's going to be a lot of comparison with this person that comes in. Unless they come in like a Michelle Obama (laughs) or, you know, that's why sometimes we're . . .

Me: Meaning? What do you mean by that? From your perspective.

Mrs. Poole: Well, she just has a lot of wisdom where she kind of knows which battles to pick and which ones not to. Or like a Martin Luther King. They're going to need people to break that ground. Or like a Jackie Robinson, everybody just saw the movie *42*. You could put certain people, Dennis Rodman, that would have failed immediately, you know? [. . .] The African American person that comes in has to clearly understand this is not about them. This is not just about black people. It's not about just . . . it's about white people coming to understand and know us too. Even though they step into that role and it's clear that there's preferential treatment in other ways, and there's absolutely none for you, are you willing to fight that battle to see, ten years from now, a more diverse Grace?

You have to decide. When Martin Luther King did that, when President Obama and Michelle Obama did what they did, when Jackie Robinson did . . . they made, and you can see that in the movie, they took that into their own spirit that they would do this for the next generation. This is not about them. That's what it's going to take, because there's nobody there at Grace now. Zero. You're starting out fresh at that school as they walk in that door. When they recruit those people, that's what they've got to be looking for.

> Somebody who's willing to help to make the change, not just somebody who's going to come to teach.

Mrs. Poole suggested that GA's administration should add another criterion to their list of qualifications for hiring black teachers: "Somebody who's willing to help make the change." Mrs. Poole also maintained that the black teachers who could successfully stay at Grace would have to make some sacrifices in order to do so. They would have to be willing to work in an environment where they would be scrutinized by parents and staff and where there would be preferential treatment based on race. They would not be able to wear their blackness too boldly (like Dennis Rodman) or be a lightning rod for change, despite whatever pride they have in their cultural background because white people need time to accept them. Mr. Armstrong, a teacher, used the term "safe" to describe the kind of black person who could make it at GA. A safe black person, he maintained, "won't rock the boat." They would have to be willing to be missionaries in a homogenous land and work hard to satisfy GA's notion of "fit" in order to change the culture for black teachers and students over time.

The black parents I interviewed were not, however, putting all of the responsibility on a hypothetical, future black teacher. They also saw themselves as important agents in GA's efforts to become more diverse. Mr. Jenkins, for instance, discussed the significance of his willingness to enroll his children in a white school:

> You have 50 million people in a room: you're going to have a Hispanic group over here, African American group over here, Chinese group over there. Everybody's going to go to their own kind, but somebody has to be willing to mingle outside of their kind to allow others to get a better understanding of who we are and what it is that we're looking for because at the end of the day, we're all looking for the same thing: we want to be loved, and we want to make sure that our needs are met, and once we're able to do that, now we can turn around and in return help other people reach that same point.

Mr. Jenkins believed that the presence of black families at GA could help others learn about the qualities that all humans have in common. Mrs. Poole and several other black parents echoed his sentiments. Mr. Baldwin made sure to assert his opinion at school meetings:

> At the end of the day, you say, "I'm going to bite the bullet. I'm going to bring up the issue. I'm going to be in every meeting. I'm going to be present. I'm going to be the change that I want to see. I'm not going to be quiet. I'm not going to sit in the back. If I have

an opinion, I'm going to state my opinion, and I'm going to be a presence there!"

He wanted to ensure that black families were both seen and heard at GA because that's the change he wanted to see GA make.

Finally, black parents had recommendations for GA in its efforts to recruit a diverse faculty. Mr. Baldwin wanted to see GA adopt an official hiring policy for diverse staff. He said, "I think that every opening should, they should consider involving people from different ethnic backgrounds . . . that becomes a policy." Mr. Curtis added, "If the person is skilled, don't pass on that person because that person is of another persuasion, and you got a few parents who are paying their money, and they're just so uncomfortable with someone who doesn't look like them." Mr. Curtis, along with other black parents, wanted to see the GA administration be willing to risk upsetting some parents by hiring another minority teacher. Several black parents also added that they wanted the administration to support the teacher against the parents once the teacher arrived.

Discussion

School leaders have an incredible power to shape how individuals in their school communities make sense of issues and events (Evans, 2007). Some administrators at GA genuinely believed and advanced the legitimizing myth that Mrs. Griffin's dismissal was not about race, even though reactions to Mrs. Griffin's choice of curriculum, dress, and demeanor suggest otherwise. Some faculty, staff, and parents did see through the myth, but many of them saw race as a largely individual reality. From their perspective, Mrs. Griffin's dismissal was something she brought upon herself through her poor choices, choices to not acquiesce to GA's racialized norms of politics, femininity, and colorblind teaching. The case of Mrs. Griffin's dismissal, however, brings into sharp relief the larger systemic issues of gender, race, ideology, and politics that formed GA's understanding of Christian unity and what it meant for a faculty member to "fit" at GA. If school administrators' sensemaking continued to be swayed by the school's vision of Christian colorblindness, which translated into the maintenance of institutionalized whiteness, GA would likely face difficulty in recruiting and retaining teachers of color.

Just as there were some minority students who found a good "fit" in terms of their shared faith at GA, one can imagine how at some point a faculty member of color could "fit" at GA. But such a teacher would likely carry a much heavier load than his or her white counterparts. In the predominantly white school Lewis (2001) studied, for example, the burden of planning Black History Month activities fell to one of the black staff members, an experience other black teachers in white schools have also had (Kelly, 2007). Indeed, black teachers and staff often experience burdens related to their race (Hall & Stevenson, 2007; Kelly, 2007; Mabokela & Madsen, 2003). Foremost, they have to prove themselves to their colleagues. "Teachers of color are often burdened," Mabokela and Madsen (2003) note, "with the psychological pressure of having to prove their worth because their expertise is often questioned by their European American colleagues, as well as by their students' parents" (p. 108). Black teachers in the Mabokela and Madsen (2003) study believed districts sought to hire teachers of color who would conform to schools' white cultural norms, even going so far as to prefer black teachers who had more Caucasian physical features, such as light skin.[13] Districts also gave preferential treatment to black teachers who were acquiescent over those who wanted to fight for equity:

> Outspoken African Americans who had an agenda of addressing racial inequities at a school were either given difficult working conditions or were isolated from other African American teachers. Those African Americans who understood the codes of power and the appropriate language and dress were more suited as the token African American.
> (Mabokela & Madsen, 2003, p. 107)

Districts rewarded African American teachers who went over and above to fit in and not disrupt the status quo. Such a minority faculty member could succeed at GA. Mrs. Griffin, however, did not because she upset GA's norms. GA's approach to diversity privileged assimilation (i.e., unity in Christ) over a recognition of difference.

Other types of predominantly white organizations also reportedly select certain types of black people for employment or admission to their institutions (Thornhill, 2018). The desired black applicants demonstrate low levels of "racial salience," which refers to "the extent to which race informs a given individual's self-concept" (Thornhill, 2018, p. 1). These organizations desire black people whom the organization determines will not increase racial tensions—they will not point out the institution's racialized practices and will assimilate to the white, colorblind culture of the organization (Thornhill, 2018). Thornhill (2018) found evidence of this practice across predominately white colleges and universities, wherein white admissions counselors screened potential black student applicants to ensure that only the "right" black students, those who wouldn't disrupt the racial status quo, matriculated (p. 14).

Similarly, Bracey and Moore (2017) found evidence of similar practices at white evangelical churches. According to them (2017), white evangelical churches maintain a "semipermeable racial boundary" in which

> white evangelicals work to be sure only a few people of color enter their churches and that those few are "the right kind of people,"

specifically those who will not challenge the racial organization of the space so that white churchgoers can continue to enjoy the white institutional space that is the evangelical church.

(p. 288)

"White institutional space," according to the Bracey and Moore (2017), is space wherein the culture, policies, and practices of the church are "normatively white" and "totalizing" (p. 284), even if the norms are rarely identified as racialized and are more commonly considered to be "race neutral" or a reflection of the organization's culture/identity (p. 285). Such a space, they (2017) maintain, results in "a robust culture that privileges whites by vesting power in white leaders' hands, populating the organization with white membership, orienting activities toward serving and comforting whites, and negatively sanctioning non-white norms" (p. 285). These spaces deter people of color from remaining in them, but even so, the practices persist unquestioned (Bracey & Moore, 2017). Further, such churches are rarely found culpable, even by the social scientists studying the phenomenon. White evangelicals, they (2017) explain, are regarded as "well-intentioned people" (Emerson & Smith, 2000, p. 1), and church segregation is typically discussed as a unfortunate outcome of different worship preferences, residential segregation, and a "natural" preference for being with one's own racial group (p. 283).

GA, then, typifies a white institutional space. When its student and faculty recruitment is analyzed, a different standard appeared for both black students and teachers that was centered on the concept of "fit." These standards required black students and teachers to more closely embody the school's norms, which limited the numbers of African Americans GA could recruit and retain. In much the same way as the school's rejection of quotas, the different standards mitigated other stakeholders' fears that more diversity would mean a decline in the academic and spiritual quality of the school. Yet the school's restriction of admission to only students of color who they believed "fit" yielded what GA would deem to be positive experiences for those students—the experience of unity in Christ. Though GA professed and often practiced a colorblind recruitment approach, it wasn't consistently colorblind, often acting in ways that were highly conscious of race.

Administrators' sensemaking about how to achieve GA's diversity goals revealed a conflict between the goals of the diversity initiative and the prevailing norms of the school, especially that of colorblindness in a "white institutional space" (Bracey & Moore, 2017, p. 284). A consideration of fit in both the admissions and hiring processes for all applicants was attractive to them since the practice allowed them (in theory) to be colorblind. However, once fit took on different standards for students and faculty of color, the practice was no longer colorblind. In fact, it suggested an additional layer of color consciousness (Thornhill, 2018).

Notes

1 Also briefly described in Blosser, 2017.
2 The National Association of Independent Schools (2016) aggregates its faculty/staff demographic data according to type of position: 15.5% of faculty, 16.6% of administrators, 31.7% of instructional support staff, and 44.6% of other staff identify as persons of color as percentages of the total number of people in those categorized positions.
3 These efforts are also briefly described in Blosser, 2017.
4 Similarly, a black mother recently alleged that a Christian school in Ohio dismissed her two children because she was not married and had them with different men (Edwards, 2019). She wondered why her children were dismissed specifically given that there were other children of unmarried parents at the school (Edwards, 2019)
5 I should note that while black parents across all grade levels chose to send their kids to GA for various reasons (for example, the school's emphasis on discipline, dissatisfaction with public schools, and academic and extracurricular opportunities for their children), all eight of the black parents I interviewed were attracted to the school's strong Christian values and believed their students could grow spiritually while attending GA.
6 GA's Application for Admission (2013) asked students to affirm whether or not they had accepted Jesus Christ as their personal savior, as well as to describe their relationship with Jesus and offer their testimony as to how they came to know him. If the student stated he/she had not accepted Jesus Christ as his/her savior, then he/she was supposed to explain why the Christian education of GA appealed to him/her.
7 I exclude the sport the student mentioned to protect the student's anonymity.
8 The omission refers to the level (e.g., elementary, middle, high) Principal Kline supervises and could compromise his anonymity within the GA community.
9 I briefly describe what happened with Mrs. Griffin in Blosser, 2017.
10 "Academic subject" refers to subjects other than PE or fine arts.
11 Teacher employment contracts stated that GA faculty must agree to try to resolve all differences with coworkers and parents in accordance with the biblical mediation guidelines established in the books of Matthew and Corinthians.
12 Dr. Smith was not using the "n-word" to denigrate a black person in this case but was rather trying to remember/describe the title of the article that the picture accompanied, which included the "n-word."
13 Young, Madsen, and Young (2010) reported a similar finding in a district they studied: "Principals believed if teachers of color did not 'sound' or 'dress' like them they would never be successful in their schools" (p. 152).

References

Anderson, G. (1990). Toward a critical constructivist approach to school administration: Invisibility, legitimation, and the study of non-events. *Educational Administration Quarterly, 26*(1), 38–59.

Bacon, P., Jr., & Thomson-DeVeaux, A. (2018, March 2). How Trump and race are splitting evangelicals. *Five Thirty Eight.* Retrieved from https://fivethirtyeight.com/features/how-trump-and-race-are-splitting-evangelicals/

Blosser, A. H. (2017). Considerations for addressing diversity in Christian schools. In D. B. Hiatt-Michael (Ed.), *Family and community engagement in faith-based schools* (pp. 33–55). Charlotte, NC: Information Age Publishing, Inc.

Bracey, G. E., & Moore, W. L. (2017). "Race tests": Racial boundary maintenance in white evangelical churches. *Sociological Inquiry*, *87*(2), 282–302.

Brown, E. (2011). "It's about race . . . no, it isn't!" Negotiating race and social class: Youth identities at Anderson school in 2005. In D. T. Slaughter-Defoe, H. C. Stevenson, E. G. Arrington, & D. J. Johnson (Eds.), *Black educational choice: Assessing the private and public alternatives to traditional K–12 public schools* (pp. 28–48). Santa Barbara, CA: ABC-CLIO, LLC.

Chan, J., & Eyster, E. (2003). Does banning affirmative action lower college student quality. *The American Economic Review*, *93*(3), 858–872.

Edwards, B. (2019, April 22). Ohio mom says kids were kicked out of Christian school because she is unmarried. *Essence*. Retrieved from https://www.essence.com/news/ohio-mom-says-kids-were-kicked-out-of-christian-school-because-she-is-unmarried/

Emerson, M. O., & Smith, C. (2000). *Divided by faith: Evangelical religion and the problem of race in America*. New York, NY: Oxford UP.

Esposito, J. (2011). Negotiating the gaze and learning the hidden curriculum: A critical race analysis of the embodiment of female students of color at a predominantly white institution. *Journal for Critical Educational Policy Studies*, *9*(2), 143–164.

Evans, A. E. (2007). School leaders and their sensemaking about race and demographic change. *Educational Administration Quarterly*, *43*(2), 159–188.

Hall, D. M., & Stevenson, H. C. (2007). Double jeopardy: Being African-American and "doing diversity" in independent schools. *Teachers College Record*, *109*(1), 1–23.

Hatt-Echeverria, B., & Jo, J. (2005). Understanding the "new" racism through an urban charter school. *Educational Foundations*, *35*, 51–65.

Herndon, M. K., & Hirt, J. B. (2004). Black students and their families: What leads to success in college. *Journal of Black Studies*, *34*(4), 489–513.

Holland, M. M. (2012). Only here for the day: The social integration of minority students at a majority white high school. *Sociology of Education*, *85*(2), 101–120.

Hughes, M. S. (1987). Black students' participation in higher education. *Journal of College Student Development*, *28*(6), 532–545.

Ispa-Landa, S. (2013). Gender, race, and justifications for group exclusion: Urban black students bussed to affluent suburban schools. *Sociology of Education*, *83*(3), 218–233.

Kelly, H. (2007). Racial tokenism in the school workplace: An exploratory study of black teachers in overwhelmingly white schools. *Educational Studies*, *41*(3), 230–254.

Kraft, C. L. (1991). What makes a successful white student on a predominantly white campus? *American Educational Research Journal*, *28*(2), 423–443.

Ladson-Billings, G. (1995). But that's just good teaching! The case for culturally relevant pedagogy. *Theory into Practice*, *34*(3), 159–165.

Lewis, A. E. (2001). There is no 'race' in the schoolyard Color-blind ideology in an (almost) all-white school. *American Educational Research Journal*, *38*(4), 781–811.

Mabokela, R. O., & Madsen, J. A. (2003). Crossing boundaries: African American teachers in suburban schools. *Comparative Education Review*, *47*(1), 90–111.

Mellowes, M. (2010). The black church. *PBS*. Retrieved from www.pbs.org/godinamerica/black-church/

Morris, E. (2006). *An unexpected minority: White kids in an urban school*. New Brunswick, NJ, Rutgers UP.

National Association of Independent Schools (NAIS). (2016). *NAIS Facts at a glance*. Retrieved from www.nais.org/Media/Nais/Statistics/Documents/NAIS FactsAtAGlance201516.pdf

National Center for Education Statistics (NCES). (2017). *Characteristics of private schools in the United States: Results from the 2015–16 private school universe survey*. Retrieved from https://nces.ed.gov/pubs2017/2017073.pdf

Newport, F. (2014, December 15). Blacks' approval of President Obama remains high. *Gallup*. Retrieved from www.gallup.com/poll/180176/blacks-approval-president-obama-remains-high.aspx

Scott, J. T. (2005). Introduction: The context of school choice and student diversity. In J. T. Scott (Ed.), *School choice and diversity: What the evidence says* (pp. 1–8). New York, NY: Teachers College Press.

Slevin, C. (2014, October 3). Controversial Colorado history plan still alive. *AP News*. Retrieved from http://bigstory.ap.org/article/5638f9e60740470db9db30b204b33a1a/history-fight-coming-head-suburban-denver

Thornhill, T. (2018). We want black students, just not you: How white admissions counselors screen black prospective students. *Sociology of Race and Ethnicity*, 1–15. doi:10.1177/2332649218792579

Yancey, G. (2006). *Beyond racial gridlock: Embracing mutual responsibility*. Downers Grove, IL: InterVarsity Press.

Young, B. L., Madsen, J., & Young, M. A. (2010). Implementing diversity plans: Principals' perception of their ability to address diversity in their schools. *NASSP Bulletin*, 94(2), 135–157.

Note: I exclude references that might in any way compromise the identity of the school.

4 Cultivating a Climate of Diversity and Unity

Beyond obtaining a more diverse faculty and student population, the other facet of Grace Academy's diversity initiative was to create a school climate that celebrated diversity (GA Diversity Statement, 2013). This goal was interdependent with GA's recruitment and retention goals. If GA's atmosphere was one in which diversity was appreciated, then the diverse students and staff GA recruited would be more inclined to stay at the school. Likewise, a diverse faculty and student body can help schools cultivate in students an appreciation for difference (Levinson & Levinson, 2003).

GA's efforts to create a culture celebrating diversity can be understood through the school's hiring of a diversity coordinator and the experiences of black students and parents. I highlight the experiences of black students and parents specifically because they were the predominant minority group at GA[1] and because their experiences were distinct from the other participants of color I interviewed, a finding consistent with other research conducted at largely white schools (Esposito, 2011; Hatt-Echeverria & Jo, 2005). Namely, black students and parents reported school experiences related to their racial identities, whereas none of the multiracial students[2] nor the one Hispanic parent I interviewed identified school experiences specifically related to their race(s). Further, blackness was associated with a distinct set of cultural expectations at GA. The perspectives and experiences of black stakeholders demonstrate what GA would need to address in order to cultivate a climate that celebrated diversity.

As with Chapter 3, I draw upon some of the central premises of CRT to guide my analysis of school culture. In addition to examining the impact of racialized norms on student of color, I also uphold CRT's tenet that the perspectives of people of color are essential for understanding the "racialized social reality" of an institution (Evans, 2007, p. 166). Thus, I feature the voices and experiences of black stakeholders prominently in this chapter.

Institutionalizing Diversity

GA administrators determined that one way to create a climate celebrating diversity was to develop a half-time position for a Christian Unity and

Diversity Coordinator. The presence of a diversity coordinator can inform a school's community that the school values diversity (Blosser, 2017; Harris, 2012). Consistent with the school's biblical approach to diversity, GA's administration envisioned a distinctively Christian approach to the position. The job description they developed included the Colossians passage[3] that underscored the diversity initiative. It also stated that the person hired would be responsible for counseling the administration and board on diversity issues, and helping to strengthen the sense of Christian unity on campus. Though the recruitment and retention of minority stakeholders were desired outcomes, the job description primarily described someone who would encourage an informed and accepting culture of diversity within a Christian context. It included several responsibilities, such as to educate and engage the community about diversity; aid and address the concerns of "specific" families; work with the administration and faculty to present "diversity awareness" in a Christian environment; create a mentoring program that helps racial/ethnic minorities integrate into the school community; disseminate job openings to "highly qualified candidates" from minority backgrounds; provide individual counsel to staff and faculty on diversity issues; develop relationships with local organizations, churches, and people who support the school's diversity efforts; strategize with the administration to recruit and welcome a more diverse school community; and help out and substitute as needed.[4] Dr. Smith was proud of this job description because it conveyed that school leaders made sense of diversity in a way that extended beyond quotas (i.e., determining desired percentages of diverse individuals); rather, it communicated that the school administration desired to educate the GA community on diversity, engage in conversations about it, and help diverse students integrate smoothly. He also felt the job's inclusion of "Christian Unity" in its title and the description's statement about the school's desired goal of strengthening Christian unity on campus reflected their conservative Christian framing of diversity and distinguished GA's approach to diversity from that of public, secular, and even other Christian schools. Much to the chagrin of the administration, though, the first diversity coordinator they hired, who was also the school's football coach, did not carry out their vision. His actions in the role ultimately reinforced stereotypical notions of blackness and led other faculty to regard the diversity coordinator position as a joke.

The Diversity Coordinator

In the early 2010s, the administration hired Mr. Wade, the school's then current football coach, to also be the Christian unity and diversity coordinator. When Dr. Smith hired Mr. Wade into that position, he hoped that Mr. Wade would be able to successfully fulfill his responsibilities as both diversity coordinator and coach. In many ways, Mr. Wade's educational background made him a logical choice for the diversity coordinator position since he majored in African American studies and early childhood education. Mr. Wade was also well respected in the Cedar Ridge community because he was a well-known athlete at his undergraduate university, and Dr. Smith felt that Mr. Wade could use his reputation to help forge relationships in the community and connect with families of color. This is not what happened.

It was clear from my interviews and conversations with Mr. Wade that his passion was coaching football. He discussed it proudly, and it dominated our discussions of diversity at GA. In fact, after my initial hour-long interview with Mr. Wade, I realized that we had mainly discussed the football team, and I hadn't learned what he did in his role as diversity coordinator. So I stopped him in the cafeteria a few days later to ask him about his role as diversity coordinator. He laughed and said, "That's a good question, a little bit of everything." When I pressed him to answer the question in greater depth, Mr. Wade said, "Really, it is about getting more diversity in the school" (field notes, April 9, 2013). He then elaborated that his job was to get black families to "chalk up" the money to send their kids to GA, which was certainly part of his job. But then Mr. Wade added, "It's sad that the only diversity in the high school is [some] black football players and one black baseball player" (field notes, April 9, 2013). I noted in my personal reflection on that conversation how ironic this seemed to me given that he was the person primarily responsible for recruiting the black football players to GA. He was also incorrect in stating that the black athletes he mentioned were the only black students in the high school, but his statement was telling in that it reinforced Mr. Wade's focus on athlete recruitment. I later began to realize how his statement also reflected the common perception at GA—that black students were all athletes.

What I didn't hear from Mr. Wade while he was describing his role as diversity coordinator was anything about cultivating a climate that celebrated diversity or educating the community, despite the roles outlined in the job description. My multiple conversations with Mr. Wade led me to see that his dual role created a conflict of priorities for him, making his job very difficult. While Mr. Wade certainly helped to increase the number of minority students in the school, it was primarily through recruiting athletes into the high school's football program. It appears that he gave little attention to recruiting students of color into the lower grades. In our various conversations, Mr. Wade explained that the school's real problem was the lack of diversity in the middle and elementary schools, but he did not claim any responsibility for the problem or offer ideas for fixing it. In fact, he explained that he and his wife chose to enroll and keep their son at a neighboring public elementary school specifically because it was more culturally diverse than GA:

> I know my son is at the Montessori School, and my wife and I want to keep him there because there's so many different cultures as opposed

to a white flight school like this, and I think we're trying to get better with that, but I think it's great for my son to be in the school. [. . .] He has classmates from Germany, Japan, from the neighboring city, from all over. He's been taught the way of the world at an early, early age.

Given the well-known challenges that racial minority students experience in predominantly white schools, Mr. Wade's choice is understandable. However, this undoubtedly placed him in an awkward position when trying to convince black families to send their kids to GA. More importantly, his job, as outlined in the job description, was supposed to be about more than recruitment. It is possible that Mr. Wade did not fully understand his job responsibilities as outlined in the job description, that he chose not to embrace them, that they had not been clearly communicated to him, and/or that the expectations placed on him in his dual roles were overwhelming and/or unreasonable. Even members of the faculty and staff were unsure of his responsibilities as diversity coordinator. Principal Beatty said to me about the school's diversity efforts and Mr. Wade, "I don't think we're at that step yet, at that level yet where we really know what's coming next or what we're expected to do. We have the diversity director, and we know he's here. We know we can access him, but I don't know what the next step is for him, and the teachers don't know either." According to Principal Beatty, then, Mr. Wade's responsibilities hadn't been communicated to staff or even all of the principals, so Mr. Wade had little accountability from his colleagues to fulfill his duties.

Another problem created by Mr. Wade's dual role as diversity coordinator and football coach was that it trivialized the diversity coordinator position. Teachers Mr. Baxter and Mr. Armstrong each noted in interviews with me that they viewed Mr. Wade's position as diversity coordinator as somewhat of a joke. They believed that the diversity coordinator title was merely a formality and said that they did not typically think about Mr. Wade as the diversity coordinator, but rather as the football coach. Mr. Baxter, for instance, described to me his attitude toward the administration's hiring of Mr. Wade as the diversity coordinator: "Don't try to pull the wool over my eyes. If you want to make him the diversity coordinator or whoever, whatever, okay, what are you doing?" Mr. Baxter continued and hypothetically asked of Mr. Wade, "Are you going out in the community? You're right here at school. You just care about your football team—bottom line!" I also observed that no one at the school used the title "Mr." when addressing Mr. Wade, as they did for most other members of the faculty and staff. Rather, faculty, staff, and students all called him Coach Wade. Thus, Mr. Wade's position as football coach and his emphasis on recruiting football players over addressing diversity in other ways reinforced the faculty and staff's perceptions that the creation of the diversity coordinator position was a superficial gesture.

The administration was not satisfied with the conflicts created by Mr. Wade's dual roles. Dr. Smith expressed his deep disappointment that

Mr. Wade did not or perhaps could not fulfill the administration's original vision for the diversity coordinator position, so he eventually relieved Mr. Wade of his diversity coordinator responsibilities, even though Mr. Wade technically retained the title and remained the football coach. While Dr. Smith still believed deeply in the position's potential, he told me that because of budgetary concerns, there were no plans to hire someone new to fulfill that position's responsibilities.

Football and Diversity

GA's decision to hire Mr. Wade as the diversity coordinator after he had already been serving GA as football coach reinforced the stereotype at GA that students of color attended GA for athletics. Specifically, faculty, parents, teachers, and students alike clearly associated blackness with football. The following statements represent the kinds of comments I heard from study participants when discussing school demographics:

> That's where we are seeing a lot of diversity come into play: the football team. I think that's true of a football team almost everywhere. Black students tend to be very good football players, and so we've seen a lot more diversity in that sport than anything else.
> (Mrs. Harper, a staff member)

> It's one of those things that this is unspoken, but obviously over the past few years, our football team is . . . we're getting more African Americans.
> (Haley, a white senior)

These comments reveal that in the minds of at least some school stakeholders, diversity at GA meant getting more black football players, affirming the pervasive stereotype of black athleticism. Interestingly, Dr. Smith and Principal Barnes pointed out that the soccer team also attracted a lot of minority students, particularly from Latin America, but that people didn't focus on Latino students when they thought about diversity because they were lighter skinned. Dr. Smith asserted, "The soccer program has been nationally ranked and that brings kids from Latin America, but people always focus on the darker color." His comment suggests that black skin and brown skin were distinct at GA, and my experiences at the school confirmed this suggestion. As an example, I repeatedly heard from GA faculty and staff that they had no teachers of color on the faculty, but there were two teachers who identified as Hispanic. One of the teachers had noticeably brown skin and taught Spanish. Yet these teachers were not recognized as being people of color because they were not black. While it was readily apparent upon visiting GA that African Americans were the predominant racial minority, the salience of blackness was also reinforced by the city's demographics. African Americans made up a third of Cedar Ridge's population, by far its largest minority group. Moreover, I noticed that GA's service opportunities were often conducted in black neighborhoods or at organizations serving predominantly African Americans, even though Cedar Ridge has a sizable poor white population as well.[5]

Dr. Smith and other faculty members explained to me how Mr. Wade's recruitment of black football players angered some white parents. Specifically, white parents complained to Dr. Smith that their children, who had been attending GA and playing football for GA since kindergarten, no longer had spots on the team because of the influx of black football players. White parents were so vocal about their concern with the blackness of the football team that I heard about their complaints completely outside of the research context when I was attending church in the community one Sunday. And in interviews, multiple participants told me that to appease white parents and other white donors, the school brokered an unofficial agreement with white parents that no more than half of the football team would be black. As one administrator reported,

> You can't have [all] black kids on the football team at a predominantly white school, so I had to sit in conversation with donors saying, "If we wanted to . . . we turn more athletes away than we accept . . . way . . . considerably more." [. . .] We know we can only keep that many and the rest are going to come up from our own program.

And such an agreement appeared to exist as exactly half of the football team was black, even if the black players saw most of the playing time. So on one hand, GA adamantly rejected quotas for the minimum percentage of diverse students, but on the other hand, the school reportedly quantified the maximum percentage of black football players it would accept.

Other schools have made national headlines for similar actions regarding the racial composition of athletic teams. For example, a former basketball coach at Bowling Green High School in Kentucky is pursuing legal action against the school for discrimination. According to the coach, she was asked to replace her African American assistant coaches with white coaches because the administration wanted the coaching staff and players to more accurately reflect the racial composition of the high school (Frakes, 2017). While selecting or dismissing coaches or players based solely on their race is discrimination, and I am not suggesting otherwise, one must also consider the possible negative ramifications of having an all-black team at a predominantly white school. An all-black team has the potential to further reinforce stereotypes about black athleticism and perpetuate assumptions that black students are only attending the school to play a given sport or make the team better. These assumptions were already in place at GA with a football team that was only half African American. Though white parents complained about the blackness of the football team, they also enthusiastically cheered on the football team at games and boasted the team's successes.[6] Football games were almost always sold out, and the people who attended them were predominantly white adults. I did observe, however, that more black families attended football games than other school events. The GA student section also rallied around the football team to such a degree that GA students won an award for being the most spirited among several other area schools.

According to school stakeholders, African American families wanted their sons to play football for Mr. Wade, so they sought him out and asked if he could help their sons get into GA. One participant explained that GA could choose the black football players it wanted because three or four times as many African American families as there were spots on the team typically inquired about admission to GA specifically for football. According to another participant, some of the selected football players received financial aid,[7] but others did not qualify because they came from families with sufficient income to pay GA's approximately $10,000 tuition.

An Unrealized Vision

The administration's sensemaking about diversity at GA resulted in the creation of a position that emphasized Christian unity and aimed to preserve the school's identity as a close-knit Christian community. The position reflected the administration's belief that doing diversity should be about more than recruiting diverse individuals, which was consistent with the school's diversity statement. Their vision for the position, however, went unrealized. And the administration's decision to hire someone as both the diversity coordinator and football coach reinforced racial stereotypes and minimized the scope of GA's diversity coordinator position so that in the minds of stakeholders, the initiative became primarily about getting good black football players to come to GA. The influx of black football players under the leadership of Mr. Wade also angered white parents and donors so much that they reportedly pressured the school to employ the very practice it so vehemently rejected: a diversity quota. The school refused to set quotas that they believed would result in the degradation of quality, especially at the expense of Christian principles, but appeared to set quotas when doing so kept donors happy and led to a good football team, regardless of the school's desire to have a more diverse student population.

Evans (2007) notes how identity and image feature heavily in school leaders' sensemaking because school stakeholders, like tuition-paying parents, scrutinize their actions as reflections on the school. This was indeed the case at GA. Despite the goals of the diversity initiative, stakeholders' sensemaking was most influenced by the need to retain the identity and image of the school as one that adhered to the prevailing norms of its white, conservative Christian context. These prevailing norms were maintained well beyond the school itself through affiliated churches, parents, alumni, the board, and the broader, southern evangelical world of the school.

The failure of the diversity coordinator position to achieve the goals of the diversity statement may have been the result of a poor hiring decision. But the selection of Mr. Wade was itself likely influenced by the school's context. When school administrators selected a well-liked and respected coach for the position, it probably became less threatening to those who may have opposed the position or the initiative. Football also appeared to be a unifying activity for GA students and families of all racial backgrounds. And achieving diversity through the athletics program fit with the racial expectations of many at the school. Black students had a "place" at GA and thus wouldn't threaten to change the culture of the whole school.

Experiences of Black Students and Parents

All schools are racially socializing institutions. That is, schools teach students the behaviors associated with belonging to one or multiple racial groups (Arrington, Hall, & Stevenson, 2003; Arrington & Stevenson, 2011; Cooper, 2011; Jay, 2003; Lewis, 2001; Pollock, 2004). The more racism students of color experience at school, the lower the students' feelings of connection to the school and the lower their self-esteem (Arrington et al., 2003). The experiences and perspectives of black students and parents brought to light the norms and values that complicated GA's efforts to create a climate of diversity and unity.

Racial Stereotyping Among Students

According to a study, the most common "race-related stressor" black students experience in independent schools is other students believing they will fulfill racial stereotypes (Arrington & Stevenson, 2011, p. 88). Of the six black students I interviewed, only the two females reported instances of being racially stereotyped at school.[8] These women were also generally more critical of GA than the black males. And I did not hear nearly as many positive comments about GA from them as I did from the black males (e.g., Elijah's claim that "GA is probably the best school you'll ever run into"). In fact, when I coded students' interviews for experiences of racial stereotypes, I discovered that no black male complained of feeling negatively stereotyped or unaccepted, unlike the black females.

Several scholars (i.e., Holland; 2012; Ispa-Landa, 2013) have reported that black females have more difficulties integrating in predominantly white schools. Holland (2012) maintains that African American males may have greater social status in white schools because they conform to positive stereotypes of them as athletic. This appeared to be the case at GA. All four of the black males I interviewed played a high-status sport (i.e., football, basketball, and soccer).[9] While both of the black females I interviewed also participated in athletics, their participation in sports did not seem to have had as positive of an influence on their school experiences as it did for the males. Holland (2012) writes that "being involved with sports and being seen as athletic (a masculine characteristic) usually brings more social rewards for males than it does for females" (p. 111). Black male students repeatedly told me how they were instantly welcomed by their teammates. I also observed the popularity of the black male football players, in particular. They were often surrounded by white females at their lunch table. A white 12th grader, Michael, described the popularity of the black male football players:

> They are loved here, and they're accepted here, and there's not anything that I think they don't like about being the only African American kids. And that's one good thing is that I think in a school that is all about people. For the most part, the . . . African American people we have here are extremely accepted, and they're not met with any . . . like, they're not pushed off the long lunch table.

A white sophomore, Carrie, told me that the black football players also received special treatment from teachers. She observed that teachers didn't ask the football players to put their phones away like they asked of all of the other students.

Yet stereotypes of black male athletes were evident. For instance, several white students brought up the financial status of football players, assuming they received financial aid. For example, Maura, a white junior, made the following statement:

> I think a lot of people are . . . since we're predominantly white, a lot of people don't like the black people that are here. I think some of that has to do with they've been recruited, and they don't have to pay as much as we have to. I don't think the students have a problem with it, but I think that parents might have had a problem with it, then pass it on to their students, because a lot of kids talk about that. Especially when they (the black football players) first got here, they talked about how they can't believe that they (GA) did that (recruited black students to play football). Because before then, we don't have any . . . maybe one or two, but then all of a sudden, our entire football team was all black guys, and they're really good. We love them

now, but what happened . . . a lot of people were like, "Who are you, and why are you at our school?"

I followed up Maura's comment by asking her how people found out that the black football players received financial aid. When she replied that she didn't know, I asked her if it was assumed. Her response was, "It might have been assumed. I think it's known that they were recruited. Some of them have said that they are on financial aid. I think some people just assumed that all of them are on financial aid. I don't know if all of them are on or not." I pressed her further:

Me: Do they say that they were recruited?
Maura: I don't know. I don't ask them . . .

My conversation with Maura reveals several assumptions. First, there is an assumption about the financial status of many of the black football players: that they receive financial aid. Then her claim that the "entire football team was all black guys" reflects an exaggerated perception of the percentage of black football players—as I mentioned, only half of the team is black. Overestimations of minority students in white schools are not uncommon (Hannah-Jones, as cited in Douglas, 2017), and the American public tends to overestimate percentages of racial minorities in the population generally (Badger, 2013). Further, my conversation with Maura reveals an assumption I heard numerous times from other students as well: that black students, especially the males, only attend GA to play sports. Here are the kinds of comments I heard from students across racial groups,

> It seems to me like kind of all the black kids who come here are mostly here just for sports and stuff. Like they (the administration) bring them in for sports and stuff, not exactly just to have them here to be diverse. For the football team, they're here to play football, not necessarily just for diversity.
> (Tina, an African American sophomore)

> For Leo and the other African Americans that are here, I don't mean to look at the obvious, but they're all here for football.
> (Michael, a white senior)

> Our football team has been recruited. And because they're black, they're really, really good.
> (Lisa, a white senior)

Lisa, in particular, also associated blackness with athleticism. In the following conversation, Maura made a similar association but elaborated

78   *Cultivating a Climate of Diversity and Unity*

that because of minority students' athleticism, GA students had expectations of them:

Me: How do you think the students would react to becoming a much more diverse school? Particularly in terms of ethnically diverse, racially and ethnically diverse. How do you think that would go over?

Maura: Probably not very well. I think maybe if we got. . . . Okay, when the football guys came for instance. We didn't like them because of their race, but we love them because they made our football team better. I think if we brought in more . . . say Mexicans or something . . . we would want something in return. Because I know a lot of people feel like they're taking something from them even though they're not . . .

Me: . . . Something in return? What do you mean by that?

Maura: The football guys, they took a lot of people's opportunity to be on the football team. Now, in return, they're giving us . . . we win the championship a lot of times. If other people come, say Mexicans . . . they're really good in soccer. If they come, they'll take our soccer team; they should win the championship for us. That's how people, how they think really. If they're going to take our opportunities away from us, you should at least do good about it.

Maura's comment reveals a stereotype that minority students only came to GA to play sports and that they were welcome to the degree that they could do something for the school (i.e., win a championship). Yet I did not hear about any of these stereotypes or expectations in the conversations I had with black male students. This may be because black males were socially benefiting from their athletic abilities, as demonstrated by their popularity in the lunchroom (Holland, 2012). Furthermore, these stereotypes were reinforced by the administration's decision to hire Mr. Wade as both diversity coordinator and football coach, and by Mr. Wade's subsequent decision to focus his attention on recruiting black football players.

On the other hand, research suggests that African American females may struggle in predominantly white schools because they are seen as embodying negative stereotypes of being "loud or hostile" (Holland, 2012, p. 116; see also Ipsa-Landa, 2013). This was certainly the case for Tina, who reported getting into an argument with a white student who called her "ghetto" in reference to Tina's supposed loudness and lack of intelligence. Denise also told me about an instance of racial stereotyping in reference to her intelligence:

> I remember I had on a Harvard sweatshirt because my aunts, like three of my aunts, went to Harvard, and someone came up to me

and, again, made a comment like, "Oh, the only way you're going to get into Harvard is because you're like on a minority scholarship and something like that." It's just comments like that that kind of can build up and get on my nerves a lot.

The student who made this comment to Denise expressed an assumption that Denise was not smart enough on her own merits to get into Harvard. The comment also reflects the belief that racial minorities get unfair advantages because of race. Belief in what white people often call "reverse discrimination" is common among white evangelical advocates of colorblindness (Emerson & Smith, 2000; Yancey, 2006). Denise went on to tell me that most of her school experiences that specifically related to her race come in the form of negative comments that she and her best friend (also black) have heard from their classmates.

Teacher Behaviors

Black students generally reported that their teachers cared about their success. But black students and parents also reported that offensive student comments sometimes went unchecked by teachers. The Curtis family shared with me that their daughters occasionally felt uncomfortable in class both because of teachers sharing their personal opinions and because of the comments of other students. Specifically, they mentioned the offensiveness of politically conservative rhetoric from teachers and students. In situations where such rhetoric offended one of their daughters, the Curtis family met with the teacher to discuss their daughter's discomfort. When I asked for an example, Mr. Curtis told the following story about his daughter:

> We had an incident with our youngest daughter. [. . .] My daughter shared with me that there were a couple of fellows who were loose spoken. They would say things, something like a young Rush Limbaugh. [. . .] It was unchecked by the instructor, by the teacher. He allowed them to do that.

Given the conservative political ethos of GA, I can see how some teachers might not have recognized the potential offensiveness of politically conservative comments. Denise told a similar story about a teacher dismissing her discomfort with another student's drawing of a Confederate flag by telling Denise, "It (the flag) was just like a southern thing." Denise explained that these are the kinds of incidents wherein she realized white people may not "get it," and so she just had to "brush [incidents] off," which is a reaction other black females have had when encountering racism in predominantly white institutions (Esposito, 2011). Incidentally, I also encountered a Confederate flag hanging in a history teacher's

80 *Cultivating a Climate of Diversity and Unity*

classroom, and when I asked the teacher if he ever got questions or comments about it from parents or students, he replied that he has "surprisingly" had very few questions or comments. He told me that he believed the lack of comments and questions was because the Confederate flag was one among many flags in the classroom and that it fit within the context of the room and subject matter. He did not consider alternative explanations for the lack of comments, such as the racial attitudes of white parents or that black students may have felt uncomfortable raising the flag's presence as an issue. While I did not interview any students who currently took classes with that teacher nor did it come up in student interviews, given Denise's reaction to a drawing of the Confederate flag, I can imagine how the flag's constant presence could create discomfort for some students and be interpreted as a racial microaggression.

There were some teachers, however, who demonstrated a unique sensitivity toward race issues in the classroom. Mr. Baxter was one of those teachers. He told me that he did not stand for racial jokes in the classroom, even if they seemed harmless. The example he offered was that once a black female joked with one of the black males about him having been in the tanning bed over the weekend. Mr. Baxter told the girl that even though the female was herself black and was friends with the male student, he wouldn't tolerate the joke because it was making someone's ethnic background the "butt" of a joke.

Despite having to sometimes brush off comments, black students loved that GA generally had teachers who cared about them, a finding consistent with other studies of black students in private schools.[10] For example, Denise said,

> We have teachers here that do care about us and care truly how we do. Because I know some of my friends in public school, not all public schools, but at least the friends I have there, they say their teachers they don't really care that much. But I know we have teachers here who genuinely care about how well we do. They really want us to be successful in the classroom. Even one was telling us, "We don't want you to fail; we want to see you do well."

Other black students echoed Denise's sentiments. Elijah, for example, took comfort in knowing that he could always talk to his teachers. I observed close student-teacher relationships as well. For example, I regularly observed teachers hugging students of all races and asking them questions about their lives outside of school.

Being One of a Few

The ratio of students of color to white students in a given school impacts minority students' academic achievement and social well-being

(Arrington & Stevenson, 2011; Esposito, 2011). Black males and females at GA reported challenges associated with being one of only a few African Americans. The Jenkins family shared with me that their daughter used to have anxiety attacks about being the only black student in her grade until another black female joined her class. Leo, similarly, explained how he decided to skip school activities because of the lack of other African Americans in his grade and at the school generally:

> Being the only African American [in his grade], of course you're going to feel singled out. I don't feel neglected, but I mean in different ways I just don't feel like as comfortable as I could because even like, the [class field] trip . . . I didn't really go on that because I'm friends with everybody in my grade, but I don't really hang around people in my grade. Like I said, I hang around the football players, and most of the football players that I hang around are [in a different grade]. The [class field] trip, I didn't go on that just because I didn't know I didn't . . . I didn't like, it wasn't I wanted to . . . I didn't think I would have that great of a time just because I wasn't with people that I like truly like . . . that I really hang around on a regular basis . . . and I just don't hang out with them.
>
> We (African American males) didn't go to school prom that they had and most of that is because the school doesn't have any African American females for us to choose from. We could bring in people from other schools, but we don't know how comfortable they will be with all like a white environment.

Leo's comments suggest that he would have felt more inclined to participate in school events if there were more black students at the school. He went on to tell me how he believes that he and the other black males at GA would feel "more comfortable" if more black students attended GA.[11] His comment about the class trip also suggests that black students tended to hang out together at school, something I observed to be true. I have numerous references in my field notes in which I observed clusters of black students sitting together at events. I asked Denise, in particular, why black students tended to hang out together at GA, and she replied, "There's not a lot [of us]. That's why." Other studies of black students in private schools have found that "the strong social bond" that African American students have in such settings are "critical to [their] academic performance and sense of identity and belonging" (Cooper, 2011, p. 228).

Leo's and Denise's experiences contrast sharply with Maura's perception of black students' school experiences. Maura, a white junior, said to me, "Well there's black people at the school, but not very many of them. The ones that are here, they are just like us—they just happen to be black." Maura, the same student who had commented that people don't like the black students for taking white students' spots on the football team, explained what she meant, which is that the few black students are like other GA students in that they aren't thugs, like black people outside of GA: "When I see a black person, unless there is someone at the school, I tend to think down on them because a lot of times those are the ones who get in a lot of trouble with gangs and stuff like that." From her perception, black students at GA are more like white students, which, in many ways, supports exactly what GA was seeking in terms of fit: assimilation to the school's existing culture, which was normed to whiteness. Yet, as Denise and Leo point out, they still recognized the ways they were culturally separate and sought the companionship of other black students at GA.

Colorblind Curricula

The school's colorblind curricula undoubtedly impacted black students' school experiences. Cooper (2011) writes, "While many predominantly white independent schools are increasingly achieving racial sensitivity in their admission process, unfortunately, they also continue to strive for racial neutrality in their institutional culture and curriculum" (pp. 226–227). This sentiment captures GA's ethos well. Even though they desired a more diverse student body, they wanted to remain colorblind in the classroom. GA's lack of culturally affirming curricular materials was quite apparent to black students. Denise, for instance, said,

> Back in eighth grade we kind of briefly went over the history of slavery because it was like American History is what we were studying. And then I know in English class we read a little short story by Langston Hughes; he's like a black author. But other than that, like Black History Month rolled around, and I was expecting at least every class to at least do something that had to do with it, either like whether we read something or did like an activity, but it like never happened.

John and I also had the following conversation in which he compared GA to the predominantly black public school he had previously attended:

Me: Are there classes in which you feel like your cultural background is affirmed? This is an example: Maybe you're reading books by African American writers or learning African American history. In your year plus here, are there classes where you feel like you're learning, or your cultural background is affirmed?
John: No. Not at all.
Me: Is that different at . . .
John: Washington (his previous school)?
Me: Yes.

John: Yes. It was pretty different because we'd usually talk about Black History Month, all of the leaders and heroes, but now we don't. Not here. We don't talk about that.

Black parents concurred. When I asked Mr. Baldwin, a highly involved black parent, if he observed any school activities that instilled cultural confidence or cultural awareness, he replied,

> I don't. Of course, it requires some thought. Just by virtue of the fact it requires so much thought, nothing comes to mind. There should be two or three things I can point to and say, "Okay, well this happened or that happened or this." I can't think of anything offhand. I just can't.

My observations and other interviews confirmed students' and parents' perceptions that GA did not offer many classroom activities that were culturally relevant to African Americans. There was an English assignment in which students were asked to read and respond to narratives by Frederick Douglas, and I heard mention of a couple of other assignments.[12] Consistent with colorblind practices, Principal Barnes suggested that if culturally relevant material was used, it wasn't used for the purpose of educating students about diversity or affirming students' cultural backgrounds, but rather because it was part of popular culture:

> There's a movie that's coming out—*42*, the Jackie Robinson story—I could see a teacher . . . if there's some literature that accompanies this and it becomes a big piece within our population and our culture, popular culture, then I would see a teacher saying "Hey, I'm going to tie into this. It's really popular, kids are loving this, it's really you know . . .," doing something like that. Our teachers have a lot of autonomy, and so I can see a teacher saying, "I'm going to tap into that and do a unit on that." [. . .] I don't know that I have any teachers [in my division] currently who look at diversity as one of the driving factors and say I'm going to use this versus this.

In a similar vein, one English teacher, Ms. Fry, reported that she skipped teaching literature from other countries, even though it was in the course text, because she wasn't familiar with it. She went on to tell me that the background of the authors "is something that doesn't matter." Teaching students to celebrate diverse voices was not one of her teaching objectives.

The intentional use of CRP,[13] however, was something black students and parents greatly desired from GA. CRP empowers minority students both socially and academically (Ladson-Billings, 1995; Milner, 2011). It also develops their cultural competence and sociopolitical consciousness so that they can better recognize and critique inequitable practices

(Ladson-Billings, 1995; Milner, 2011). Accordingly, Denise believed that culturally relevant material would unite students across racial differences at GA, because black students "can feel a little bit of a separation because it's more white kids and then less black kids." And black students and parents generally believed that *all* students would benefit from CRP because it would make them more culturally aware and help to combat the racial stereotypes they may hold.

Further, black parents and students wanted GA faculty and staff to talk openly about racial issues with each other and with students. Mr. Jenkins said, "I think the school needs to be willing to face the race issues head on and not act like it doesn't exist when those type of things do pop up that cause that racial divide." Similarly, Denise wanted to see the school discuss the biblical understanding of race to help combat stereotypes and prepare kids for the diversity in the real world. She explained to me how when out in public, some of her white GA friends immediately assumed that black men were "thugs." Maura's comments from earlier confirms this. Denise's solution was for the school to have open conversations about race grounded in Christian theology:

> I don't think that they really come out and say we're, from a biblical standpoint, like we're all one under God's eyes. They don't try to emphasize that enough here. They kind of put it, I guess, under a blanket. They kind of just choose to ignore it, rather than talk about it and stuff. And they think that ignoring it would make the situation better, but it really doesn't. It just kind of keeps things sustained. And if they would probably talk about it more, then I think it would probably get better, but they don't, so everyone kind of keeps doing the same thing every year.

These kinds of conversations, however, would conflict with the school's belief in colorblindness, though not its diversity statement's affirmation of unity in diversity. Arrington et al. (2003) claim that a school's refusal to discuss racial issues openly is "detrimental" to all students in its community, but especially its black students (p. 3). Moreover, they (2003) affirm Denise's observation by stating that faculty and staff member's "discomfort and silence" in discussing race and racism does not preclude students from having negative school experiences related to their race (p. 3). The authors (2003) add, "Not talking about race and racism does send messages to members of the school community. Not discussing race and racism, particularly when it is in the form of denying their relevancy, also leaves notions of privilege and whiteness unexamined" (p. 3). Essentially, denying the relevance of race preserves the status quo and communicates the value placed on the status quo to stakeholders of color. On the other hand, discussing race and racism can greatly improve the schooling experiences of students of color (Arrington et al, 2003; Ladson-Billings, 2006; Lewis, 2001; Pollock, 2004; Singleton & Linton, 2005). As Lewis (2001) states, if a community is truly committed to racial equity, "It is essential to talk about how race operates even in settings where people say it is not important" (p. 804).

Several of the black parents I spoke with mitigated GA's lack of race talks, lack of culturally relevant material, and low black student enrollment by racially socializing their students at home. Research shows that the racial socialization black students receive from their parents can allay the negative social and academic effects of the race-related stress they experience in schools (Stevenson & Arrington, 2011; Neblett, Philip, Cogburn, & Sellers, 2006). For example, all but one of the eight black parents I interviewed told me that they attended predominantly black churches as another means of socializing their kids.[14] The Pooles and the Jenkins similarly encouraged their children to supplement their GA education by reading books by minority authors. And the Poole family made sure their children were sufficiently exposed to other African Americans outside of school by sending their son to camp every summer at a nearby historically black university. When I asked the Pooles why they felt it was important to make sure their kids were exposed to other African Americans outside of school, they said it was because the real world is diverse. Then they went on to explain that GA needed to become more diverse because learning occurs when people are exposed to diverse people and experiences. They believed that a more diverse population would benefit white kids more than black kids. "Our kids (meaning black kids) are going to get what they need through parents," Mrs. Poole said. She continued, "It's the white kids that are just losing. They're losing a full perspective of other people who don't look like them. That's the reason diversity needs to be more at Grace. Not for our black children."

Despite GA's goal to create a climate in which students can celebrate their differences, GA did not intentionally cultivate this climate through its curriculum. Some black students and parents, though, believed that doing so would help build unity in diversity, as well as help students combat the racial stereotypes they held.

Discussion

From the CRT perspective, school leaders, faculty, and staff must evaluate racialized norms, attitudes, practices, and minority student experiences as they seek demographic change so that they can cultivate a climate that affirms minority students who come to the school (Evans, 2007; Lewis, 2001). The experiences of black students and parents at GA, coupled with the school's failed initial efforts at hiring their first diversity coordinator, demonstrate the real impact racialized norms, attitudes, and practices can have on students' schooling experiences, especially students of color.

Blackness was clearly associated with athletics at the school, which likely influenced, even as it was influenced by, the decision to hire the football coach as the school's first diversity coordinator. Not talking about race at GA reinforced the school's colorblind attitude and suggested to black students, albeit unintentionally, that the racial stereotypes and social isolation they were experiencing were not valued. Moreover, the modicum of culturally relevant material in the curriculum sent the message that people of color have made few valuable contributions to society and contributed to at least one black student's feelings of exclusion. In addition, the low percentage of black students at GA precluded some black students from participating in school events and connecting with their classmates. Black students did, however, appreciate the care their teachers showed them, and black male athletes, in particular, appeared to have few negative experiences related to their race.

As a teacher educator, I know it is possible to cultivate a climate emphasizing unity in diversity without having to practice colorblindness. In other publications (i.e., Blosser, 2017), I have outlined biblical rationales that Christian schools could adopt for acknowledging student differences. I have also offered suggestions for culturally responsive activities that fit within a conservative Christian framework.[15] But as a teacher educator, I can also imagine the possibilities if GA practiced "culturally responsive caring", a practice that Geneva Gay (2010) describes as "focus[ing] on caring for instead of about the personal well-being and academic success of ethnically diverse students" (p. 48). Gay (2010) goes on to explain that "while caring about conveys feelings of concern for one's state of being, *caring for*[16] is active engagement in doing something to positively affect it" (p. 48). The key phrase in her explanation is "active engagement." Black student and parent experiences at GA suggest that the faculty and staff could become more intentional and explicit in engaging race (thereby abandoning colorblindness), and in so doing, they would come closer to achieving their goal of cultivating a climate that celebrates differences. Such efforts could then be supported by a Christian Unity and Diversity Coordinator whose responsibilities are clearly defined and prioritized in the school community. But as one black GA parent, Mrs. Curtis, put it, for any of these efforts,

> the school has to have the courage to stand up to whatever parent that comes through the door, regardless of what kind of money they have, or what kind of influence, and say, "We're doing this because this is the right thing, and it's the right thing that God would have us do."

Having that courage would be GA's challenge.

Notes

1 Black students comprised over half of the 9% of students who identified as persons of color.

2 The minority students I interviewed (n = 9) identified only as either African American (n = 6) or multiracial (n = 3). I did not, for instance, interview any student who identified solely as Hispanic or Asian.
3 Colossians 3:11: "Here there is no Gentile or Jew, circumcised or uncircumcised, barbarian, Scythian, slave or free, but Christ is all, and is in all."
4 I briefly mention the diversity coordinator position and its responsibilities in Blosser, 2017.
5 See Chapter 5 for more on service at GA.
6 During the football season I observed, GA's football team won a state title in its division.
7 Administrators and a staff member in admissions/financial aid were quick to explain to me that GA did not offer any athletic scholarships because that would violate NCAA regulations for K–12 schools. Rather, football players had the same opportunity as any other student to apply for financial aid based on their family income. I was also assured that football players did not get any preferential treatment in receiving financial aid.
8 Stereotypes are also briefly described in Blosser, 2017.
9 When I asked a GA staff member to recommend black males I could interview who didn't play a sport, they recommended John. I came to discover that John played a sport; the sport just wasn't football. This event reaffirms just how prevalent associations of blackness and football were among GA staff. Moreover, I could not identify a black male, non-athlete to interview.
10 Arrington et al. (2003) found that 56% of black students in independent schools believed that the teachers cared for students.
11 See (Blosser, 2017, p. 46) for Leo's exact quote about feeling "more comfortable."
12 Teacher Mrs. Fry mentioned that another teacher covered the Harlem Renaissance in class. She also mentioned that an American Literature class covered works by Harriet Jacobs. Likewise, a parent, Mrs. Marshall, told me that her son read *Roll of Thunder, Hear My Cry* and studied Harriet Tubman in middle school, though I believe these were in Mrs. Griffin's (GA's first black teacher, as described in Chapter 3) class, so I cannot assume these activities were a regular part of the middle school curriculum.
13 Culturally Relevant Pedagogy refers to a model of teaching that uses students' cultural practices and backgrounds to engage them in learning, and it aims to build cultural competence and raise students' critical consciousness about inequities in their world (Ladson-Billings, 1995).
14 It is quite possible that the one exception attended a predominantly black church as well, but she did not reveal that in her interview with me.
15 See Blosser, 2017.
16 My emphasis.

References

Arrington, E. G., Hall, D. M., & Stevenson, H. C. (2003, Summer). The success of African-American students in independent schools. *Independent School Magazine*. Retrieved from www.nais.org/Magazines-Newsletters/ISMagazine/Pages/The-Success-of-African-American-Students-in-Independent-Schools.aspx

Arrington, E. G., & Stevenson, H. C., Jr. (2011). "More than what we read in books": Black student perspectives on independent schools. In D. T. Slaughter-Defoe, H. C. Stevenson, E. G. Arrington, & D. J. Johnson (Eds.), *Black educational choice: Assessing the private and public alternatives to traditional K–12 public schools* (pp. 78–90). Santa Barbara, CA: ABC-CLIO, LLC.

Badger, E. (2013, October 22). American's vastly overestimate how diverse the country really is. *City Lab.* Retrieved from www.citylab.com/equity/2013/10/americans-vastly-overestimate-how-diverse-country-really/7320/

Blosser, A. H. (2017). Considerations for addressing diversity in Christian schools. In D. B. Hiatt-Michael (Ed.), *Family and community engagement in faith-based schools* (pp. 33–55). Charlotte, NC: Information Age Publishing, Inc.

Cooper, R. (2011). Enhancing the schooling experience of African American students in predominantly white independent schools: Conceptual and strategic considerations to developing a critical third space. In D. T. Slaughter-Defoe, H. C. Stevenson, E. G. Arrington, & D. J. Johnson (Eds.), *Black educational choice: Assessing the private and public alternatives to traditional K–12 public schools* (pp. 222–233). Santa Barbara, CA: ABC-CLIO, LLC.

Douglas, D. (2017, December 14). Are private schools immoral? A conversation with Nikole Hannah-Jones about race, education, and democracy. *The Atlantic.* Retrieved from www.theatlantic.com/education/archive/2017/12/progressives-are-undermining-public-schools/548084/

Emerson, M. O., & Smith, C. (2000). *Divided by faith: Evangelical religion and the problem of race in America.* New York, NY: Oxford UP.

Esposito, J. (2011). Negotiating the gaze and learning the hidden curriculum: A critical race analysis of the embodiment of female students of color at a predominantly white institution. *Journal for Critical Educational Policy Studies, 9*(2), 143–164.

Evans, A. E. (2007). School leaders and their sensemaking about race and demographic change. *Educational Administration Quarterly, 43*(2), 159–188.

Frakes, J. (2017, October 10). KHSAA investigating bowling green boys basketball team for recruiting violations. *Courier Journal.* Retrieved from www.courier-journal.com/story/sports/preps/kentucky/2017/10/10/khsaa-investigating-bowling-green-boys-basketball-recruiting-violations/751539001/

Gay, G. (2010). *Culturally responsive teaching: Theory, research, and practice* (2nd ed.). New York, NY: Teachers College Press.

Harris, D. M. (2012). Diversity in the Christian school. In T. P. Wiens & K. L. Wiens (Eds.), *Building a better school: Essays on exemplary Christian school leadership* (pp. 197–211). Stoney Brook, NY: Paideia Press.

Hatt-Echeverria, B., & Jo, J. (2005). Understanding the "new" racism through an urban charter school. *Educational Foundations, 35,* 51–65.

Holland, M. M. (2012). Only here for the day: The social integration of minority students at a majority white high school. *Sociology of Education, 85*(2), 101–20.

Ispa-Landa, S. (2013). Gender, race, and justifications for group exclusion: Urban black students bussed to affluent suburban schools. *Sociology of Education, 83*(3), 218–233.

Jay, M. (2003). Critical race theory, multicultural education, and the hidden curriculum of hegemony. *Multicultural Perspectives, 5*(4), 3–9.

Ladson-Billings, G. (1995). But that's just good teaching! The case for culturally relevant pedagogy. *Theory into Practice, 34*(3), 159–165.

Ladson-Billings, G. (2006). From the achievement gap to the education debt: Understanding achievement in U.S. schools. *Educational Researcher, 35*(7), 3–12.

Levinson, M., & Levinson, S. (2003). "Getting religion": Religion, diversity, and community in public and private schools. In S. Levinson (Ed.), *Wrestling with diversity* (pp. 90–123). Durham, NC: Duke University Press.

Lewis, A. E. (2001). There is no 'race' in the schoolyard: Color-blind ideology in an (almost) all-white school. *American Educational Research Journal, 38*(4), 781–811.

Milner, H. R. (2011). Culturally relevant pedagogy in a diverse urban classroom. *Urban Review, 43,* 66–89.

Neblett, E. W., Jr., Philip, C. L., Cogburn, C. D., & Sellers, R. M. (2006). African American adolescents' discrimination experiences and academic achievement: Racial socialization as cultural compensatory and protective factor. *Journal of Black Psychology, 36,* 199–218.

Pollock, M. (2004). *Colormute: Race talk dilemmas in an American School.* Princeton, NJ: Princeton UP.

Singleton, G. E., & Linton, C. (2005). *Courageous conversations about race: A field guide for achieving equity in schools.* Thousand Oaks, CA: Corwin Press, Inc.

Stevenson, H. C., & Arrington, E. G. (2011). "There is a subliminal attitude": African-American parental perspectives on independent schools. In D. T. Slaughter-Defoe, D. J. Johnson, E. G. Arrington, & H. C. Stevenson (Eds.), *Black educational choice: Assessing the private and public alternatives to traditional K–12 public schools* (pp. 64–77). Santa Barbara, CA: ABC-CLIO, LLC.

Yancey, G. (2006). *Beyond racial gridlock: Embracing mutual responsibility.* Downers Grove, IL: InterVarsity Press.

Note: I exclude references that might in any way compromise the identity of the school.

5 A Hidden Curriculum of Diversity

Students learned about diversity at GA, but for the most part, they weren't learning as a result of GA's intentional efforts to teach them about diversity. I saw few efforts to create culturally relevant assignments, and the activities I observed that could be considered culturally relevant, like the school's International Missions Fair, were intended for purposes other than educating students about diversity. Diversity learning, in other words, was an unintended outcome of many of GA's regularly planned activities, despite the school's intentional efforts to make every member of the school community feel that their cultural background was celebrated (GA Diversity Statement, 2013). As evidence that diversity teaching and learning were unintentional, consider Principal Barnes's response when I asked him to identify activities that I should observe related to diversity:

> Within a normal instructional context within a normal school day, I don't know that I would have anywhere to send you. Now you know we do some service things that touch that more diverse population. I mean, you can go into this classroom that has six minority students, but we're not going to be doing anything in that classroom that is dedicated to diversity.

In other words, GA wanted its students to feel their unique backgrounds were celebrated but wanted to achieve that without any specific programming or lessons around diversity. This explains why when I asked Principal Westerly the same question as Principal Barnes (which school activities I should observe that might relate to diversity) he likewise could not point me to any specific diversity-related activities. He responded instead with, "I think it (diversity) is more implicit." Principal Westerly also doubted that GA was an appropriate research site for me because he believed I wouldn't find anything to write about. The principals' responses imply, and my observations confirm, that most diversity-related teaching and learning was embedded in activities that served some other purpose. Only months into my data collection, I recorded in my field notes my frustration with finding out about school events that could have been relevant to diversity only *after* they happened. I made a note to myself stating, "I think this is evidence that these events are not developed for any sort of diversity-related purpose" (field notes, May 10, 2013). And this implicit learning reflected the community's belief in minimizing attention to difference.

Hidden Curriculum and Sensemaking Defined

According to Principal Westerly, adopting a diversity initiative afforded GA administrators, faculty, and staff with an opportunity to review how its existing practices were teaching students about diversity. As Principal Westerly put it, "It's almost because we're looking for means of diversity [that] we're basically reinterpreting what we're already doing." Jay (2003) argues that as schools adopt multicultural initiatives, it is important that they critically examine their existing policies and practices in order to uncover the ways in which they reinforce hegemonic norms and values, and inadvertently stifle multicultural efforts. Hidden curriculum refers to the implicit lessons students learn in school through policies, practices, interactions, structures, etc. (Blosser, 2017; Bowles & Gintis, 1976; Esposito, 2011; Jay, 2003; Lewis, 2001). In her study of a predominantly white school, Lewis (2001) explored the way students learned about race through the school's hidden curriculum. She (2001) notes how "uncovering the many implicit and explicit racial lessons that are 'taught' and learned in schools involves not only studying the curriculum, but also studying the explicit racial discourse of the community and the implicit logic that shapes practices" (p. 782). She (2001) explains how schools frame and convey messages about race via their policies, practices, and personnel, and "conclude[s] by making a case for broadening our focus on transforming schools beyond multicultural curriculum to include all racial practices and lessons conveyed in both explicit and implicit ways by all members of a school's community" (p. 783). Similarly, Esposito (2011), in her study of a predominantly white university, found that students learned lessons not only about race, but also class and gender, from the interactions they had with other students and professors. She termed this the "hidden curriculum of diversity" (p. 145). In this chapter, I define the "hidden curriculum of diversity" as the implicit lessons that Grace Academy students learned about identity via the school's policies and practices.

During my time at GA, it became apparent that all members of the school community (administrators, faculty, staff, and students) were making sense of diversity. Specifically, they were making sense of diversity messages that were both implicitly and explicitly embedded in the school's policies and practices (Blosser, 2017). Stakeholder sensemaking is particularly enlightening to an examination of a school's hidden curriculum because sensemaking is largely concerned with coming to understand that which isn't immediately evident (Weick, 1995). Weick (1995) reasons that it is the lack of that which is evident that distinguishes sensemaking from interpretation:

> When people discuss interpretation, it is usually assumed that an interpretation is necessary and that object to be interpreted is evident. No such presumptions are implied by sensemaking. Instead, sensemaking begins with a basic question, is it still possible to take things for granted?
>
> (p. 14)

Rarely is the hidden curriculum of schools immediately evident—hence, it bears the term "hidden." Though scholars do not often analyze the sensemaking of students in their analyses of organizational change and meaning-making,[1] the sensemaking of students can communicate meaningful information about a school's hidden curriculum. Not only can student sensemaking help identify a school's hidden curriculum, but it can also reveal what students are actually learning from the school's policies and practices, regardless of the policies' or practices' intended purposes. Student sensemaking about diversity thus features prominently in this chapter.

GA's Hidden Curriculum

On a daily basis, GA engaged in numerous practices that conveyed a hidden curriculum of diversity. For example, I discussed in a previous chapter how GA's lack of culturally relevant curricula communicated that the contributions of people of color were not valued. Likewise, the gendered behaviors of GA's teachers communicated that males were the protectors and women were modest and submissive. And then there was the association between diversity and athletics that was reinforced by Mr. Wade's position as both football coach and Christian Unity and Diversity Coordinator. In this chapter, though, I focus on three practices through which students learned about diversity: service opportunities, GA's Policy on Biblical Living, and the biblical framing of curricula.[2] I highlight these three practices because students frequently identified them as sites for learning about diversity, even though that was not the primary purpose of any of the practices. Moreover, these three practices shared a common purpose that reflected the school's ideology and mission: to help students become strong Christians.

Service Opportunities

GA was like many other public and private K–12 schools, as well as colleges and universities, who are increasingly providing opportunities for students to serve their communities (Blosser, 2012). Many schools have good intentions in providing volunteer opportunities and view offering the opportunities as a "win-win" situation for students, the school, and community partners (Eby, 1998; Slimbach, 2000). But while schools are quick to consider the positive outcomes of student volunteering, they often fail to carefully consider the possible negative consequences of their service projects, like reinforcing deleterious conceptions of the persons ostensibly served (Eby, 1998; Slimbach, 2000).

Volunteer opportunities were a big part of the culture of GA. In fact, I discussed service with 49 of 60 participants in the study. At the senior awards ceremony, several students qualified for the President's Freedom Award, which required a minimum of 100 hours of volunteer service (observation, May 16, 2013). And there was hardly ever an open slot on sign-up sheets for service projects. According to faculty and staff, GA offered different types of service opportunities. Some of the opportunities were providing someone with something they needed (i.e., food, clothing, supplies). Other opportunities centered on providing a service for someone (i.e., building a house, cleaning). And then there were mission opportunities that involved evangelizing and often included a service component. GA was passionate about and eager to provide mission opportunities for students, so when the staff coordinated volunteer opportunities, they frequently involved a mission component. When Dr. Smith explained the importance of mission-driven service opportunities in a faculty meeting, he explained that he didn't want students to go off to college having never shared Christ with anyone (observation, September 9, 2013).

Service opportunities imparted GA's hidden curriculum of diversity because they taught students about diversity, even though that was not an intended purpose for offering them. The stated purpose of providing volunteer opportunities was to help students develop socially and spiritually, or as they claimed in their publications, to give students the chance to live out their faith. Principal Westerly said that offering volunteer opportunities "could have simply been a means of ministry that had nothing to do with diversity." One staff member, Mrs. Bishop, asserted that diversity learning was an "added benefit" of volunteering. And Principal Barnes explained that the purpose of service opportunities was to give students the chance to share their faith and that exposing them to diverse people and environments was a "result" of that.

Though part of the hidden curriculum, the diversity learning that occurred through service projects was significant because of the sheer amount of service that occurred across all grade levels. Also, 19 of the 20 GA students I interviewed identified service opportunities as one of the primary school activities through which they learned about diversity. Through these opportunities, students processed many facets of identity, including socioeconomic status, race and ethnicity, religion, gender, ability, and age.[3] For example, I accompanied third graders on a trip to a retirement home to hand out Valentine's cards that the elementary school students had made for the residents (diversity of age). I joined middle school students on an afterschool trip to evangelize, play with kids, and provide and serve dinner to several hundred people in a predominantly black, low-income community (diversity of race, ethnicity, and socioeconomic status). And I accompanied high school students on several service trips, including volunteering for Special Olympics (diversity of ability) and serving a meal and performing praise music at a community center (diversity race, ethnicity, and socioeconomic status). I also attended a school-wide service day called Disciples' Feet. At this event, students, staff, and parents washed the feet of the people in the community just as Jesus did as described in the book of John. Then GA students, staff, and parents gave the person new shoes (diversity of race, ethnicity, socioeconomic status).[4]

There were other service opportunities as well. Throughout the year, the GA community constantly collected items to be donated to others, such as cans, health products, coats, purses, etc. The school had monthly commitments with two different organizations to provide and serve meals for the communities the organizations served. Students regularly volunteered with Miracle League, a baseball league for individuals with physical disabilities, and they hosted dances for adults with cognitive disabilities. Each spring, the entire high school got a day off from school to clean up a Christian summer camp. And every summer for many years, GA took a group of high school students on a mission trip to the Dominican Republic. In the Dominican Republic, they evangelized in a town square, repaired houses, and spent time with residents in orphanages and homes for people with disabilities. These are only a sample of the many service projects and trips GA offered.

For some of the students, participating in service projects helped them to modify their assumptions about various groups of people. For example, Maura, a white junior, volunteered at Disciples' Feet, and she explained how that experience was the first time she ever interacted with "people like that," referring to poor African Americans. Maura said that before volunteering, she assumed the "people like that" were all too lazy to get jobs and that they relied on government funding to buy drugs. In interacting with them, though, Maura explained how she learned that her assumptions were wrong and that, in fact, many of the "people like that" were trying to find jobs but couldn't because of tough economic times and that the scarcity of jobs was beyond their control:

> I think when we were giving them shoes, at first I was just like, "Wow, they should. They get drugs—they can buy their own shoes." Then afterwards, I realized that a lot of them are trying. A lot of them just can't find jobs because of the economy and stuff. A lot of them . . . they don't have any control over that type of stuff.[5]

Through participating in Disciples' Feet, Maura realized that poverty was a problem larger than the individual and that perhaps fault laid in the system. Maura's revelation was particularly noteworthy because her prior attitude toward poor, minority individuals was typical of both middle and upper income white communities and white, evangelical Christians (Emerson & Smith, 2000; Hatt-Echeverria & Jo, 2005). These communities believe that social problems, such as racism and poverty, are created and sustained by individuals, not societal or governmental structures (Diangelo, 2018; Emerson & Smith, 2000; Hatt-Echeverria & Jo, 2005). Yancey (2006) notes how "from an individualist point of view, racial economic disparity," in particular, "can be the result of the sins of African Americans" (p. 21). Thus, Maura's sensemaking about diversity marked a possible transition from an individualist understanding of poverty (i.e., poor people are poor because they are lazy) to a structuralist understanding of poverty (i.e., poor people are poor because we have an economic system that makes it difficult for them to seek and find employment that pays a living wage) (Diangelo, 2018; Yancey, 2006). Maura also went on to tell me how she connected the service experience with a sermon her pastor had recently delivered in church about the church's responsibility to be a mother to the homeless. She said that making that connection "was God's way of telling me that [I] need to be servant oriented."

Maura wasn't the only student for whom serving helped to change an assumption. Elijah, an African American student, told me how he learned an important lesson about race through interacting with both white and black men at a halfway house while volunteering there with the football team. He said,

> We went and spoke with them, and they spoke with us, and they taught us. [. . .] They were different races; they weren't just all African American, [or] all white race. It was mixed, so it showed us that race doesn't determine your lifestyle.

Elijah's realization that race does not necessarily dictate one's life trajectory was important given Elijah's identity as an African American male. Moreover, service opportunities that could debunk racial stereotypes were especially noteworthy, since many of the service projects at Grace appeared to involve serving "disadvantaged black people," to use the words of Mrs. Stanley, an African American parent.[6] Mrs. Stanley believed that many of GA's service opportunities sent the wrong message about racial minorities, and she wanted to see service opportunities in multiracial communities that would instill positive lessons about race. It is also significant to point out that both Maura and Elijah's service opportunities allowed students the chance to have meaningful interactions with the people they were serving. Those interactions gave voice to the marginalized, and the students who listened learned powerful lessons.[7]

Some of GA's service projects, however, tended to reinforce deleterious conceptions of the other, an outcome of service that is well-documented in literature (e.g., Blosser, 2012; Eby, 1998; Slimbach, 2000). Dr. Smith, for one, wasn't convinced that all of the service projects GA participated in sent the right message. He explained to me his frustrations with a project the school participated in that involved cleaning up a predominantly black neighborhood. He felt that the project sent a message to the black community that the school thought they were dirty, and it reinforced for students the stereotype that black people were dirty. Slimbach (2000) uses the term "benevolent paternalism" to describe the attitude of many Western Christians who go into communities and try to make those communities live up to Christian standards (p. 1). Dr. Smith was frustrated that the faculty members who planned such projects didn't recognize the potentially damaging messages the projects could communicate to students.

As another example of problematic learning outcomes from serving, students reported realizing that they were "blessed" while serving others. For example, Lisa, a white 12th grader, said of her experience serving at Disciples' Feet, "So like it makes me reflect on how blessed we are here." To evangelical Christians, realizing one's blessedness while serving others may be perceived as positive or innocuous, especially if the server recognizes their privilege and/or genuinely believes God provides his/her blessings (which are generally understood to mean things like money, abilities, etc.). But recognizing one's blessedness only in contrast to the marginalized bespeaks the assumption that the other person is less blessed by God. Such perceived "blessedness" creates a deficit perspective of the other and an unequal power dynamic between the server and the served (Slimbach, 2000). Further, as Eby (1998) writes,

> "by defining needs as deficiencies, students are able to separate themselves from the problems they encounter. They fail to see that often the same social structures which work well for them create the needs in the communities in which they [serve]."
>
> (p. 4)

In other words, realizing one's blessedness in the face of need can reinforce individualist understandings of social problems and preclude the sort of realization Maura had about societal structures: that the very structures that provide my "blessings" prevent others from having access to such "blessings."

At its extreme, Principal Barnes lamented that some students went into or completed service projects believing that they were saviors, a sentiment I heard from some students when they explained how proud they were to share Jesus with people on service and mission trips. Chance, a white senior at GA, described his experience in the Dominican Republic in a way that exemplified the savior mentality:

> Being able to go somewhere like that where they almost seem to have no hope and bring Jesus to them and bring that hope to them and that sense of happiness and love-like that was just probably one of the best parts.

When students are led to share Jesus in marginalized countries or communities, they can mistakenly assume that poor people aren't already Christians or that their poverty is due to a lack of Christ (Slimbach, 2000). These assumptions lead students to believe that they are the saviors, casting the poor as deficient, sinful, or even damned.

Other students I spoke with, however, gained an understanding of blessedness while serving that recognized the strengths of the people served instead of their deficits. For example, Elijah reflected on all of his service experiences, and while he recognized that he was blessed, he also recognized that the people he served were blessed: "Other people are blessed in different ways that you may not understand." Brandon, a mixed-race senior, and Davy, an African American sophomore, similarly admired the happiness of the poor people they served. Brandon even thought that the Dominicans he met while serving there were better Christians than most of the people he knew. He noted, "They (the Christian Dominicans) actually go out in the community, and they help people. They live out their faith." Principal Barnes explained the kind of attitude he wanted students to develop though serving others: "You may have more than some of these people economically, but they may have some advantages that you don't have as well."[8]

Michael, a white 12th grader, pointed out another complexity of GA's mission-oriented service projects. He expressed concern that such service projects seemed to become more about how the project impacted the student serving than the person being served. Michael described his view of the school's mission-oriented service projects:

> Because everyone that comes back from that Dominican Republic trip . . . There's always a presentation in the first few assemblies or chapels of the year, and they never focus on what they accomplish. In fact, I never hear what they actually accomplish in this mission trip to the Dominican Republic. It's always like, God just taught me that this is how I'm supposed to care for people, and it's like an eye-opening experience to the person who went, but as to what they actually accomplished for these people. That's why I think it's kind of . . . and it may well be that they do tons of stuff there and that they actually do help, but it's certainly obvious that that's not the

focus. The focus is on this kind of inner faith fulfillment kind of idea, and it's less obvious with some things like the Disciples' Feet, [which] I think was a great success in the sense that we raised a lot of money. We have a lot of people who didn't have shoes and needed shoes, but I think the goal of it is more based on a kind of faith idea or fulfillment of this faith, and it's kind of a thing that you're called to if you are a Christian, and that's kind of where I think a lot of the outreach comes from. I wish there was more, some more organizations, some volunteer organizations that are more after, I think, actually accomplishing things for the people who need it. Personally, I've done things like Habitat for Humanity, who builds houses.

Michael observed that GA often emphasized students' spiritual growth from volunteering over the service they accomplished. I confirmed the accuracy of Michael's observations in both my interviews with students who went to the Dominican Republic and in my field notes about the chapel service devoted to the Dominican Republic trip. I recorded that the centerpiece of the Dominican Republic chapel session was when students walked across the stage holding up a piece of cardboard with their testimonies of what they learned about God, Christ, sin, etc. from going on the mission trip (observation, September 12, 2013). And when students who had been to the Dominican Republic discussed the trip in our interviews, they emphasized how much they grew spiritually more than they emphasized the work they accomplished. But while Michael saw GA's emphasis on spiritual growth as problematic, it is important to acknowledge that such growth was in line with GA's purpose for providing service opportunities.

Religious organizations often emphasize self-growth in framing mission trips (Slimbach, 2000). And Slimbach (2000) notes that Christian organizations would do well to acknowledge this as they sponsor mission trips. Specifically, they need to recognize that when Jesus sent his disciples to various communities, "his sending was expressly not about providing the messengers an unforgettable experience. [. . .] It wasn't primarily about the goers; it was about the receivers" (p. 4). Eby (1998) likewise attests that the often "mixed objectives" of service carried out within educational institutions "has the potential for prostituting service" by making the project meet the needs of the students or the school, rather than the community being served (p. 3).

That said, some students learned from service opportunities that service has the potential to benefit both server and served. Mark, a mixed-race senior, for example, explained how through service,

> We're taught to celebrate diversity. We're also taught to . . . we're also taught about unity; uniting with groups that are different from us, educating ourselves about their conditions, their beliefs, and

working with them so that we can have mutual improvement, for both ourselves and other communities as well.

Mark's realization in many ways represents the ideal learning outcome for GA—he learned unity in diversity and the importance of working with, not for, others.

GA's hidden diversity curriculum was embedded in the service opportunities it provided to students. Students' sensemaking about diversity was thereby framed by GA's purpose in offering service—spiritual growth. That said, the lessons students learned through service were inconsistent and were at times even contradictory. More importantly, service opportunities were not universally teaching students to celebrate diversity within a framework of unity in Christ, one of the stated goals of the school. Thus, as schools evaluate service opportunities with diversity in mind, they should consider if the messages students are learning are the messages that they want them to receive. After all, students' sensemaking about diversity revealed that some of the lessons they were learning, like a structural understanding of social problems, while aligned with the perspectives of some people (e.g., Critical Race Theorists), may not be aligned with the beliefs of the school community.

Policy on Biblical Living

School policies often serve to maintain the status quo (Jay, 2003). They are also important sources of information about cultural norms and expectations (Jay, 2003). School policies that are designed to regulate students' bodies and behaviors, in particular, can convey messages to students about the school's expectations for their race, socioeconomic status, and gender (Morris, 2006). Based on my research at GA, I am adding sexual orientation to Morris's list.

On the same page of GA's student handbook as its policy that required nondiscrimination against "students of any race, color, national and ethnic origin" was GA's Policy on Biblical Living. This policy stated the school's biblical obligation to work with parents in molding Christ-like students. The policy outlined the behaviors and attitudes it deemed to exemplify Christ-like living. It stated the school's right to deny admission to or withdraw an enrolled student whose behavior or home life stood in opposition to the school's understanding of Christ-like living. The behaviors listed included identifying as LGBTQ, practicing homosexuality, supporting sexually immoral acts, or not feeling able to accept the biblical values of the school.

The Policy on Biblical Living served several purposes at GA. Through it, the school established its right to withdraw or deny admission to a gay student or a student whose parents were gay. Likewise, it supplemented other school documents, like the dress code, by defining the school's understanding of Christ-like behavior. It also designated activities that the school did not consider to be Christ-like. In so doing, the policy sent a clear message to students that living a Christian life was incompatible with being gay or even supporting people who are gay. Because the policy allowed students to be denied admission or withdrawn from school, it also communicated that Christian communities should be sexually pure and that the wrong kinds of difference infect, pervert, and warp the community, a belief historically rooted in the Christian practices of shunning and excommunication.

When the expectations communicated via GA's Policy on Biblical Living affected a student's enrollment at GA, students identified it as an important moment of diversity-related learning at GA. It is notable that students identified this student's experience as related to diversity because GA did not specifically recognize sexual orientation as a God-given facet of identity that would qualify one as diverse. That students identified the following moment of learning about sexual orientation as related to diversity suggests that they conceptualized diversity more broadly than GA's administration. In fact, five students told me in interviews the same story about a gay student who left GA. Three of them mentioned it to me completely unprompted when I asked them to tell me any diversity-related story at GA, again indicating the significance of the event for students' diversity-related sensemaking at GA.

Here's the incident as it was related to me: In the year prior to my study, a gay high school student enrolled at GA, which I was told was an uncommon occurrence. The student had been out (at least on social media) prior to arriving at GA, so rumors quickly spread about him in the first few weeks of school. After a few weeks of attending GA, the student came out to his peers at school. When Dr. Smith and the other principals got wind of the student's admission, they called a meeting with the student and his parents. The student's parents, Dr. Smith told me, were "very strong Christians." In the meeting, Dr. Smith explained that GA's official stance was that acting on attractions to the opposite sex is "not God's design" but is a choice and a sin. Dr. Smith explained that the school was willing to work with a student who admitted he/she was struggling with acting on his/her homosexual inclinations and was willing to seek help in resisting those inclinations. Dr. Smith added that GA would not, however, work with the student who said (in Dr. Smith's words), "I am this way. I'm going to stay this way." What Dr. Smith meant was that GA would not continue to enroll a student who was going to continue acting on his/her sexual inclinations toward a member of the same sex. Dr. Smith likened the situation to keeping a student who said, "I'm a cheater; I'm going to keep on cheating," or "I'm a thief and I'm going to keep on stealing." From GA's perspective, a continued bad behavior warranted a conversation with parents and the student. The administration gave this student a chance to think about whether or not he was struggling with acting on his sexual orientation and would seek help with his struggle, but after a few days, the student told the school he simply was gay and didn't wish to pursue help with it. Thus, the administration counseled the family to withdraw their son from GA, which they did.

After the student withdrew, school administrators never discussed the situation with the student body in any kind of organized forum, so students were left to make sense of the situation on their own. From the students' perspective, GA dismissed the student, as opposed to what actually happened, which is that the student's parents withdrew him with the support of GA's administration, a distinction Dr. Smith claimed to be quite significant. For instance, Michael, a senior, told me that "all of the students were talking about this (the student's dismissal)" and were asking if the school, "honestly kick[ed] him out because he's gay?" Mark, a senior, said of students' response to the school's decision, "We were all ashamed and shocked. He was a really nice guy. He was extremely genuine, and he was down to earth." When I asked Mark why students were ashamed and shocked, he responded, "Just because we hold kind of a different attitude than the administration." My limited data confirms that Mark was generally right. Four of the five students who shared this story with me disagreed with the school's decision to ask the student to withdraw. Haley, a senior, was the only student who felt that the school handled the situation appropriately:

> It was handled in the right way for it was made clear, "Okay, this is what we believe, and so if you're going to be a part of Grace, then it would make sense that you wouldn't openly try to tell everyone else that that's not true." [. . .] But just in the same sense, we wouldn't let a girl walk around however she wanted [to be] dressing and that's her freedom.

Haley's attitude reflected GA's in that she believed the mere presence of the student would threaten the religious beliefs or sexual choices of other students attending Grace. She also saw acting on same-sex inclinations as a choice akin to a girl selecting her clothing. Lindsay and Mark, however, accepted that practicing homosexuality was a choice and a sin, but both adamantly disagreed with the school's rationale and decision to support the student's withdrawal. They disagreed with GA's rationale and decision because they believed that if the gay student had stayed at Grace, he would have had the opportunity to learn, in Mark's words, that "homosexuality is not the right choice" and could stop "living that way," an opportunity the student would not have in a secular or public school. Lindsay, a senior, put it this way:

> Like, being in that Bible class, he could have realized, "Oh, wait, this is not right. This is not how it should be." And I think, say, if he went

to a public school after that, what is he going to learn? He's going to learn, "Oh, wait, that Christian school kicked me out, or asked me to leave." And I really disagree with them asking him to leave. [. . .] I mean, it's not going to—I don't know what they're worried about, if it's with people at our school turning homosexual. That's not going to happen. The odds of that happening or him not turning, him becoming . . . I don't know, non-homosexual, then like, the odds are more in his favor of not being homosexual.

Lindsay and Mark believed that GA students and staff would have been a good influence on the gay student and could have potentially helped him choose to stop engaging in homosexual behaviors. Lindsay's comment also revealed her concern over the gay student's perception of Christian schools (and by default, Christians) after being counseled to withdraw. Michael shared Lindsay's concern and told me that he felt the school's actions were "contradictory" to the Christian ideal of acceptance. Lindsay and Mark also suggested that even students who may have regarded practicing homosexuality as sinful were willing to accept a gay student, even as they hoped for or encouraged him to change.

Anthony, a senior, described students' reaction to the student's sexual orientation. He explained that among the student body, there was a "hesitant acceptance" of the student's sexual orientation because many students felt they should accept him, but they were afraid that if they did, other students and teachers might believe they weren't Christian, which "is almost like a death sentence here at Grace." Anthony went on to tell me how he was personally reluctant to share with his GA teachers and peers his openness to learn more about controversial issues (like gay rights) because he knew his openness was counter to the school's teachings. As he described the school, "I mean it's just like, you're just assumed to be a Christian, exert certain principles, and if you don't, you just kind of get looked down upon." Anthony's perspective suggests that GA's pervasive culture of purity and conservative Christianity was more powerful than the strategies it employed to celebrate difference.

A teacher I interviewed shared a similar perspective to Anthony's. The teacher was reluctant to share with his colleagues his confusion about the sinfulness of practicing homosexuality. Perhaps his reluctance was because his job depended on his acceptance of the school's stance on homosexuality.[9] Perhaps he also feared social ramifications from his colleagues. Regardless of the reasons for his reluctance, this teacher asked me for reassurance of his anonymity in my study, and then he confided in me that he had a gay brother. He explained that he didn't fully understand how to reconcile his faith and his brother's sexual orientation:

> I haven't really figured out a good time yet or a good way to say, "I know God made you this way, and I know God does not make junk, and I know he's given you the ability, though, that even though

he's made you like this, it doesn't mean that you have to act on it. But I know he doesn't want you to have a miserable life either." It's just so hard. It's so hard, and I don't even know if I fully understand it.

This teacher, like Mark, Lindsey, and Hailey, understood that acting on homosexual feelings was a choice, but for the teacher, it was a choice that didn't entirely make sense. Choosing not to practice homosexuality, according to the teacher's reasoning, might resign his brother to a life a misery, a life he couldn't imagine God wanting for his brother. The teacher added that attending a school with such a strong stance on homosexuality also made it difficult for his children to understand their favorite uncle's sexual orientation: "My . . . kids now know (that their uncle is gay), and they're struggling with it. They don't get it, especially being at a Christian school like this. It's very hard."

The teacher and students' sensemaking about GA's policy may reflect a larger societal shift in the attitudes of evangelicals toward issues related to sexual orientation. According to the Public Religion Research Institute, from 2004 to 2014, evangelical support for gay marriage has gone from 10% to almost 25%, and that number jumps to nearly 50% among evangelicals under the age of 35 (Francis & Longhurst, 2014). GA students were influenced by secular messaging about what diversity means since they regarded sexual orientation as a category of identity when the GA administration did not. From the GA administration's perspective, then, the fact that GA students had a broader conception of diversity than they did could be a rationale for more explicitly defining and teaching students about diversity, assuming that they want to guide students' thinking about sexual orientation and sexual practices.

Regardless of changing attitudes in the larger evangelical community, GA's Policy for Biblical Living accomplished, in part, its goal: students recognized the school's expectations about their sexual behavior and religious beliefs concerning sexual orientation. And many students accepted the school's theological stance, even as they rejected the way the policy was implemented to determine who could and could not attend Grace Academy. The school's overt stance, which was communicated through this policy, also stifled some students' and at least one teacher's ability to feel safe asking questions about and/or exploring issues related to sexual orientation. And it reportedly created emotional strife for students with gay family members. Undoubtedly, the policy shaped how students made sense of sexual orientation and other sexual attitudes, and it reinforced the cultural hegemony of conservative Christianity and heterosexuality at GA.

Worldview Curricula: The Not-So Hidden Curriculum of Diversity

Conservative Christian ideology framed all subjects taught at GA. Diversity learning in the classroom, thus, occurred within that framework. In

104   *A Hidden Curriculum of Diversity*

this section, I discuss how students learned about various worldviews, including religious ones in the classroom. I focus on worldviews because the differences between worldviews were addressed (and this term was explicitly used) in many courses at GA, including social studies, science, psychology, and religion. Teachers used the conservative Christian worldview to frame discussions of all other worldviews. I observed that teachers taught students to identify the flaws in non-Christian worldviews and the strengths of the Christian worldview in an effort to demonstrate the "truth" of the Christian worldview. The underlying message was that non-Christian worldviews were less complete than the Christian worldview. Admittedly, some of the diversity learning that occurred within GA's worldview curricula was not hidden—that is, teachers explicitly taught the differences between various worldviews. But I chose to include worldview curricula in a chapter on hidden curricula because the primary purpose of teaching students about different worldviews was not to teach students to recognize the inherent value of the worldviews, as might be the case in a secular multicultural curriculum. Instead, the aim was to make the Christian worldview appear as the most consummate worldview among other worldviews. Like with service opportunities and the Policy for Biblical Living, the purpose of worldview teaching was to strengthen students' Christian identities, not to teach them about diversity so that they could celebrate differences. Moreover, GA did not adopt their worldview curriculum in response to the goal in its strategic plan to prepare students for the conflicting Christian and secular viewpoints they would encounter outside of GA. In fact, GA faculty had been teaching students about worldviews in one course, Understanding the Times (UTT), for over 20 years. Like with service opportunities and GA's Policy for Biblical Living, however, students identified courses in which they learned about worldviews as significant sites of diversity learning at GA. I found that students learned about diversity not only from the courses' content but also from the manner in which various worldviews were presented to them.

The premise of UTT was that students needed to learn about diverse worldviews in order to be prepared to live and evangelize as Christians in the real world. UTT is a widely used curriculum in Christian schools. It teaches students about six prevalent worldviews: Christianity, Postmodernism, Marxism, New Age, Cosmic Humanism, and Islam. Students learn how each worldview approaches the following disciplines: theology, biology, psychology, philosophy, ethics, sociology, political science, economics, history, and law. At GA, students were required to take UTT in the 12th grade and an abbreviated form of it in the 8th grade. When I asked students in focus groups to identify the classes in which they learned the most about diversity, both focus groups agreed that UTT was by far the course that taught them the most about difference. I found it interesting that students mentioned this religion/philosophy course as the one in which they learned the most about diversity, as opposed to a course in which they (sometimes) read works by ethnic minorities or learned about other cultures, like social studies, foreign language, or English. It suggested that students had learned to think of diversity largely in terms of religious difference (despite the fact that the GA administration did not include religious difference among the God-created facets of identity in its diversity statement). This finding is echoed in other studies of Christian schools (e.g., Schweber & Irwin, 2003; Wagner, 1990, 1997). Further, my observations of many GA courses confirmed students' identification of UTT as the course that most intentionally emphasized diversity (in the form of religious/worldview difference), as no other courses I observed emphasized any facet of diversity on a regular basis. For example, the English courses I observed only occasionally included works by minority authors (e.g., Frederick Douglas) or works engaging feminism (e.g., Ibsen's *A Doll's House*), and social studies courses only topically engaged issues like slavery and voting rights. UTT, conversely, compared worldviews and religions on a daily basis.

The primary purpose of UTT, according to curricular materials and GA students and faculty, was to enable students to recognize Christianity as the superior worldview and to be able to "defend" it against other worldviews. Miller (2018) explains that evangelical Christians tend to become defensive about their faith because "certainty is often revered as better than doubt or questioning" and, therefore, "any counterpoint, any varying belief, is seen as an attack on Christian values as a whole." GA students explained that they had to be prepared to defend their views because when they entered the "real world" (i.e., the world outside of GA), they would be attacked for their views and called bigots because of their beliefs. Thus, UTT's agenda was largely concerned with Christian identity preservation. Chance, a senior, used violent rhetoric to describe how UTT prepared him for an attack on his Christian worldview in college:

> During that class, [the teacher] gives us so many examples of real-life examples from his college experience. He gets people to come in all the time and talk about their college experience. He prepares us a lot for, like, when your professor is bashing Christianity or something like that, or just shoving evolution down your throat or something, how to approach that and how not to bash them, but just tell them what's going on and what you believe in.

Summit Ministries (2018), the publisher of the UTT curriculum, uses similar language of defense and power to describe the curriculum: "No other Bible course so effectively equips students to engage their culture and defend their faith with sound biblical theology and powerful apologetics." GA teachers and students alike told me that Christians were better prepared to defend their worldview if they were armed with an understanding of other worldviews and how people holding other worldviews might critique Christian viewpoints. To prepare students to defend themselves, one of the objectives of UTT (as stated on the course syllabus) was that a student should learn to "articulate a factual foundation for his/her chosen worldview." While that statement implied an openness to let students decide which worldview to adopt, another one of the course objectives revealed that Christianity was the worldview the course was promoting: "After completing this course, the student should be able to garner dust from Christ's feet on his/her robe as he/she lives out God's truth and extends his glory." Mr. Tate, one of the school's UTT teachers, told me that he would be disappointed if a student became Muslim at the end of UTT because that would mean the course was not effectively taught.

I learned from attending the first few days of UTT that the most important document in the class was a chart that students were required to memorize. The chart had the six worldviews listed across the top and the ten disciplines listed down the side. It provided a few words to summarize each worldview's perspective on each discipline. This chart was designed to help students easily spot similarities and differences among the various worldviews. For example, students were supposed to recognize that Islam and Christianity shared perspectives of both biology (creationism) and ethics (moral absolutes), but differed in their perspectives on sociology[10] and history.[11] Consistent with GA's framework of unity in diversity, Mr. Tate emphasized commonalities between the worldviews and explained that finding commonalities between worldviews was particularly important for preparing students to engage the culture outside of GA and spread the gospel. He also believed that finding points of commonality with various cultures was how Paul began to spread the "good news" in the Bible:

> I suppose when I first started teaching the class, I was most fascinated with the differences between the worldviews, and the longer I've taught it, I find the commonality between some of the disparate perspectives to be the most intriguing thing. Not that I want to be a Universalist by any stretch. I'm a Christian, but I want to find common ground from which I can relate to other members of the human race, because that's what I see Paul doing in Acts. I see him going to reason with people on the basis of their commonality. I don't see him going into the culture and saying here let me smash you to pieces with my evidences for the historical resurrection of Jesus. He meets them on their own turf. He goes and says to the Epicureans and the Stoic philosophers in Rome, I see you have some statues, and I see that you like to sit around and talk about ideas, and I see you have gods, and I see you have a statue to an unknown god. Can I offer a suggestion as to who that might be? Right? . . . I try to encourage our

students to find those common denominators and relate to the people in our culture out of those places.

But Michael, a senior, found problems with the way those commonalities were emphasized via the chart's one-word descriptors. As he described it,

> The first thing: it gives them a key word. It breaks everything down, to what Postmodernists believe about sociology, into one word. It's got it in a chart. That is made to . . . you have to be able to memorize that. That framework, which I think sets you up for a lot of misconceptions and misinterpretations, is very much instilled at the beginning.

Michael elaborated that neither the chart nor the rest of the UTT curriculum accounted for variation within each major worldview. For example, he explained how the Christian worldview he was taught reflected only the beliefs of conservative Christians, which excluded varying Christian viewpoints, like those of Catholics and mainline Protestants. The implicit lesson of the chart was that followers of a given worldview/religion were monolithic in their thinking.

UTT's chart, Michael claimed, also represented the way controversial issues and diverse ideas were generally taught at GA: "There's a black and white answer to everything. Either right or wrong, and everything that's in gray is nonexistent. No one here, no teacher, would let you consider a gray area." He further stated that at GA "there is no value in anything but evangelical Christianity." Michael accurately interpreted UTT's message of right and wrong because Summit Ministries (2018) currently advertises their UTT curriculum in terms of good and bad by stating, "Understanding the Times surveys today's major worldviews and teaches students how to identify and counter the bad ideas so many young adults have unwittingly adopted."

Further, Michael's impression that GA privileges the conservative Christian worldview throughout its curriculum was also on point. I discovered that in AP Biology, for example, students were taught the theories of both evolution and divine creation, even though divine creation was not included in the College Board's standard AP curriculum (College Board, 2013). In teaching these theories, GA teachers emphasized fallacies in the theory of evolution while they offered evidence of divine creation. Students were instructed, however, to argue in favor of evolution on the AP exam, even if they didn't believe in it so that they could pass the test. GA faculty and administrators believed that the benefits of opening the school to secular culture and offering AP courses outweighed the consequences that came with having to teach students the secular perspective on subjects. The rationale was that since students were going to learn secular perspectives on subjects in college anyway, then at least GA faculty could control how learning about diverse worldviews occurred, which was through a conservative Christian frame.

Much like Michael, Anthony, a junior, struggled with the school's approach to teaching diverse worldviews and religions. He and I discussed how he learned about Islam in a different class:

Anthony: ... I mean we had Bible 1, where we discussed Islam and some of those things. But it's from a Christian perspective, so it's kind of like going immediately off the basis that it's wrong rather than understanding what it is exactly and then letting you come up with your ideas about it.

Me: Okay. In learning about Islam in that way, what do you think about that experience?

Anthony: I think it's good that they're being or many people are being exposed to other religions because GA is very, kind of secluded and cut off from the real world. But I don't think they should teach it off the basis that it's immediately like you teach it, presenting it as if it is wrong. I think they should just like present the information for what it is and then allow the student to figure out that it's wrong by themselves rather than just telling them it's wrong.

Anthony valued GA's efforts to teach about diverse worldviews, but he desired a less prescriptive approach to teaching them. Instead, he wanted the opportunity to form his opinions about various worldviews, rather than being told what he should believe. Anthony and Michael, then, resisted the way GA was shaping their sensemaking about religions and worldviews. Specifically, they resisted the message that all non-Christian religions and worldviews were inherently monolithic and wrong.

But other students, like Amanda and Jan, both seniors and conservative Christians, seemed to accept GA's message that there were right and wrong beliefs and behaviors. Amanda described what she learned about sexual orientation in UTT:

> You can't accept everything, because if you're against being gay or lesbian or whatever, bisexual, transsexual, whatever, you can't be for it by saying, "Oh what's up, Kate? You're doing it!" When you say that, you're basically saying, "Well, okay then. I'm for it for you but not for it for me." But you can't say that. You're either for it, or you're against it. There's no middle way for a topic such as that because since we're talking about that . . . just in the Bible it says one man and one woman. If you are for that for someone else, well then what is that saying about you?

Jan likewise said of what she was learning in UTT: "It actually is teaching me to look at the world, and I got to be like, oh, that's wrong or that's not true, because this is what the Bible says, and this is what Christ has told us." As GA taught them, Amanda and Jan relied on the authority of scripture to interpret ideas they encountered. They weighed ideas in terms of right and wrong because they learned that for conservative Christians there were moral absolutes and that justifications for relativism were unconvincing.

Michael and Anthony's discomfort with GA's pedagogical emphasis on Christian "truths" becomes more understandable when one considers that neither Michael nor Anthony identified as conservative Christian, making them religious minorities in the school. They identified as mainline Protestant and Catholic, respectively. Accordingly, their viewpoints were not representative of all students (as demonstrated by the contrasting viewpoints of Amanda and Jan). They seemed to have more trouble with GA's approach to teaching than the conservative Christian students I interviewed, and for both of them, their religious identities as non-conservative Christians shaped how they made sense of what and how they were learning. Anthony's experience as a Catholic, for example, made him aware of the angle with which GA approached many subjects, but particularly the critical view with which it approached religious beliefs that were aligned with something other than conservative Christianity. He told me that students made incorrect assumptions about his faith and viewed Catholicism negatively. Michael similarly explained how his religious minority status shaped his learning experience at GA:

> I accepted the challenge of being in a hostile environment to open views to further my own understanding of this culture. In a sense, I've been immersed in a culture that is not my own, that I don't identify with, completely. I'm not on the opposite end of the spectrum, but I'm certainly differentiable from a lot of the things that happen here. I blamed it on . . . this challenge has been great. I think it's been very healthy for me to have to consider a lot of things that I would never have probably considered had I gone to a high school where I was just like, "Oh, you know, some of your views, we're not that worried about it." I think because there has been this level of "this must be your view" and whatever, that I didn't jump and started looking into things that I don't think I would have had I gone to a school that was more open, if you will.

As a non-conservative Christian, Michael found himself reacting to GA's prescriptive interpretations of others' worldviews. He took an interest in and felt compelled to research issues further, which he said he might not have felt he needed to do had the school taken a more neutral stance. Thus, one cannot simply conclude that GA's approach was uninspiring. In fact, both Michael and Anthony supplemented their GA education by reading books outside of school and researching issues on their own, activities that many parents and educators would praise. Anthony said that he and other like-minded friends at GA also started a debate club as a way to explore and help other students explore perspectives other than the ones GA taught them. He explained how he and his friends recognized "that there's more to a side than just the Christian perspective," and that a Christian defense of views may be limiting when engaging other people in the real world. Sticking to his Islam example, he elaborated:

> They (the teachers) don't say Islam is wrong because the Bible says. I mean they give valid reasons, but I don't know. It's still kind of coming from like the assumption of using the Bible. I mean when you're debating with an atheist or someone, you can't really use the Bible to back up any because they don't believe in it.

Anthony's argument reflects the sentiments of philosopher, Richard Rorty, who claims religion to be a "conversation stopper" when people use it as a rationale for their positions on issues (Kunzman, 2015, p. 80). Those who are hostile or resistant to religion may well reject positions grounded in religious beliefs (Kunzman, 2015). Through forming a debate club and researching multiple sides of issues, Anthony was able to mediate the one-sided messages he was receiving at GA and prepare himself for future conversations with people who may not accept theologically based rationales for arguments.

Research confirms that other Christian schools have similar organizational ideologies and pedagogical approaches. Schweber and Irwin (2003), for example, observed that the religious ideology in the fundamentalist Christian school they studied so strongly influenced both students' and teachers' reading of Holocaust history that students refused to consider alternative explanations of the Holocaust. The Holocaust unit Schweber and Irwin observed focused on persecuted Christians, not persecuting Christians, and it attributed Jews' oppression during the Holocaust to their historical rejection of Jesus as savior. The teacher offered no avenues to explore other causes of the Holocaust, such as racism, anti-Semitism, or economic conditions. Peshkin (1986) similarly found in his ethnography of Bethany Baptist Academy that he did not "see students learning that dissent and compromise are critical attributes of a healthy democracy, rather than unwelcome guests in the house of orthodoxy" (p. 296).

GA's approach to and its alteration of the AP Biology curriculum, in particular, is relevant to both historical and contemporary educational debates in the US. Over the past few years, a group of politically conservative school board members in Colorado argued for changes to the AP US History curriculum. They wanted the curriculum to "promote citizenship, patriotism, essentials and benefits of the free enterprise system, respect for authority and respect for individual rights" and to not "encourage or condone civil disorder, social strife or disregard of the law" (PBS, 2014). School board members wrote letters to Christian

A Hidden Curriculum of Diversity 111

conservatives urging them to join the district's curriculum review committee, knowing that Christians would likely agree with their criticisms of and recommendations for the curriculum (Mehta, 2014). The College Board stated in response to the situation that if a district refused to teach some of the central ideas in an AP course, the course would lose its AP designation (Brundin, 2014). Similarly, the Texas State Board of Education sparked major controversy when it voted in November 2014 to approve new US history textbooks that emphasized politically conservative and Christian readings of history (Associated Press, 2014; Isensee, 2014). Specifically, some of the books that were up for approval "exaggerate[d] the influence of the Bible, suggest[ed] that taxes deliver no benefit to society, and argue[d] some segregated schools really were 'separate but equal'" (Nelson, 2014).

In one instance, I observed a similar sanitized presentation of history at GA. I attended an event where guest speakers were invited to speak to the fourth grade about life during the Civil War since they were covering the Civil War in social studies. The speakers arrived in costume (one man was dressed as a Union soldier; another man was dressed as a Confederate soldier, and a woman was wearing a fancy gown and bonnet) and carrying guns and bayonets. The students were enthralled. But I noted to myself that I was shocked how not once in the hour-long presentation did the speakers mention slavery as part of life during the Civil War, nor did they claim slavery as a cause of the Civil War. The speakers claimed that states' rights versus a unified government was the reason for the war. While the social studies teacher had taught slavery as one of the causes of the Civil War, as well as the significance of the Thirteenth and Fifteenth Amendments (observation, April 25), I was worried that what students would remember about the causes of the war was what the speakers presented given that they made such an impression on the students.

Understanding the explicit and implicit lessons communicated in GA's curricula can inform contemporary policy debates surrounding standardized curricula. Most importantly, how the content of courses is framed can communicate as much as the content itself. Student sensemaking about various worldviews was framed in a particular way so that one worldview, the conservative Christian worldview, always appeared to be the right one. This messaging was consistent with GA's conception of diversity. GA's stance was that religious identity was of utmost importance provided that one identified as a conservative Christian. Other religious identities were not to be celebrated because they were wrong. Some students, like Michael and Anthony, found themselves resistant to the school's approach and its presentation of non-Christian worldviews as wrong. Their experiences suggest a need to further research the experiences of religious minority students in religious schools. From what I observed in UTT and from interviewing students, though, the majority of GA students were like Amanda and Jan in that they accepted the school's stance, meaning they have or will graduate from GA holding the dominant conservative Christian perspective that the worldviews of all non-Christians are flawed. In this sense, GA successfully carried out its mission of teaching all curricula through a conservative Christian frame, which espoused moral absolutes and the superiority of its worldview over all others.

GA's success in framing all subjects through a conservative Christian lens raises an important policy question. Some scholars might argue that openness to the ideas and beliefs of others is necessary for participation in a democratic society and/or civil life (i.e., Gutmann, 1987; Peshkin, 1986). As Peshkin (1986) says about religious communities that view truth in absolutist terms,

> The true believer's inflexible, inexorable doctrinal yardstick, which so readily sorts out right from wrong and good from bad, is the basis of an incivility which both denies and defies the social complexities of our society. It is the antithesis of that live-and-let-live outlook which at its best derives from genuine respect for, if not thoroughgoing joy in, the diversity of others.
>
> (p. 290)

Thus, one could ask that if students begin attending schools like GA with public dollars (i.e., vouchers), should the recipient schools be required to promote an openness to worldviews and religions other than conservative Christianity?

Discussion

GA's emphasis on students' spiritual growth, coupled with its belief in minimizing attention to difference, meant that students learned about diversity inadvertently through policies and practices designed to strengthen their Christian identities. Research suggests that GA may not be atypical in this respect. For instance, in the Christian school they studied, Schweber and Irwin (2003) found that teachers taught students about Judaism and the Holocaust not because teachers felt such information was important knowledge, but rather because teachers felt learning about those subjects might make students stronger Christians. As they (2003) describe one teacher,

> Primarily, Mrs. Barrett saw the import of the Holocaust in its relevance to her identity as a Christian, and she hoped that learning about it would bolster her students' Christian identities. [. . .] If the Holocaust itself was not an interesting or important subject matter on its own terms, neither was any other history or any other subject matter in the school curriculum. Rather, all were subsumed into the

A Hidden Curriculum of Diversity 113

work of building a strong Christian identity in each student and thus building a strong collective of Christians with a shared memory.
(pp. 1700–1701)

GA taught students about worldviews and offered them service opportunities for the same reason. And school policies, such as the Policy on Biblical Living, were designed to encourage and preserve students' Christian lifestyle as they defined it. Yet all along the way, students were making sense of diversity through these activities.

Table 5.1 presents the disparate and sometimes contradictory diversity messages GA students received from each of the activities discussed in this chapter.

The table is telling. On one level, the messaging of GA's hidden curriculum of diversity was inconsistent. What this inconsistency reveals is the danger of having a diversity curriculum that is hidden rather than explicit. GA couldn't control what students were learning about diverse others. But to teach about diversity explicitly would require GA to expand their definition of diversity to include facets of identity such as sexual orientation since students clearly had a wider conception of diversity in this regard than the school leaders did.

At another level of analysis, the table shows commonalities between the messaging of these three practices. An analysis of the commonalities reveals that GA's hidden diversity curriculum conveyed one very prominent diversity message: the most important identifying characteristic was one's religious identity. And this message fit the school's mission. Hence, students were encouraged to evaluate their spiritual growth from serving others, to practice the behaviors that constituted a Christ-like life, and to recognize the rightness of Christianity in comparison to other worldviews and religions. GA's hidden diversity curriculum also suggested that diversity education looked different at conservative Christian schools than it did at public or secular private schools.

GA set a goal for itself to create an environment wherein students could celebrate their differences, but that goal is likely misleading for those outside of conservative Christianity. At GA, students learned to comprehend differences from a conservative Christian perspective. So GA did not want to teach students to celebrate differences that the school didn't consider to be created by God in its diversity statement (i.e., sexual orientation and religious difference).[12] In regard to these kinds of diversity, students primarily learned through GA's hidden curriculum of diversity that their duty as Christians was to convert, avoid, or oppose LGBTQ individuals and non-conservative Christians. GA missed some opportunities to forward the goals of its diversity initiative by leaving so much of its students' diversity learning hidden. But one can only understand what GA meant by diversity—and their goal to teach students to celebrate it—if one uses a conservative Christian lens.

114 *A Hidden Curriculum of Diversity*

Table 5.1 Disparate Messaging of GA's Hidden Curriculum of Diversity

Service Opportunities	Policy for Biblical Living	Worldview Curricula
• Service is a way to live out Christian faith • Service is about my (the server's) personal and spiritual growth • Service allows us to unite with diverse others for mutual improvement • I (the server) am the savior for the poor • Problems such as racism and poverty may be perpetuated by social structures, not merely individuals • Poverty and racism are problems individuals bring on themselves • Poor and/or minority people can be joyous and can be blessed by God • I (the server) am more blessed by God than those I serve • Poor and/or minority people are better Christians than the people I know • Poor people aren't Christian • Poverty is caused by a lack of Christ • Race doesn't necessarily determine one's life trajectory • Poor and/or minority people are deficient • Black people are dirty	• Being gay and/or supporting people who are gay is incompatible with living a Christ-like life • Homosexual inclinations and/or behaviors are sinful and acting on one's inclinations is a choice • Christian communities should be pure, and the wrong kinds of difference will pervert those communities • Students are welcome at GA only insofar as they embody GA's ideals • Confusion about and/or openness toward sexual orientation is unwelcome at GA	• Conservative Christianity is the best worldview/religion among all others • Conservative Christianity is right. Other worldviews/religions are wrong • Worldviews are monolithic and followers of them typically believe the same things • Conservative Christianity is under attack • Knowing the premises of other worldviews will prepare you for an attack on Christianity • Knowing the premises of other worldviews will prepare you for Christian evangelism • Sometimes you have to lie about your beliefs in order to satisfy those in secular culture • There are only truths and untruths, right views and wrong views • Conservative Christians use the Bible to defend their positions on issues, but such a defense may be limiting

Notes

1 Gilmore and Murphy (1991) and Phillippo, Brown, and Blosser (2018) are notable exceptions.
2 I briefly mention GA's Policy on Biblical Living and its service opportunities in Blosser, 2017.

A Hidden Curriculum of Diversity   115

3 I did not observe nor hear mention of encountering diversity in terms of sexual orientation, so I did not include it.
4 Also mentioned in Blosser, 2017.
5 Maura's quote and an abbreviated analysis of it also appear in Blosser, 2017, p. 45.
6 My observations of service events support Mrs. Stanley's observation.
7 Blosser (2012) and Eby (1998) caution, however, that while relationships are important vehicles for positive learning, schools should be wary of the broken relationships short-term service can involve, particularly for marginalized populations and children who have seen too many people care for them and abandon them.
8 Recognizing the strengths of others can be encouraged through the intentional framing of service projects (Blosser, 2012).
9 Every faculty and staff member was required to sign an employment contract stating that they accepted the school's stance on sexual orientation. Further, all employees had to agree that engaging in sexual acts the school deemed immoral, such as premarital sex or extramarital affairs, homosexuality, viewing pornography, and child sexual abuse, were grounds for dismissal. Finally, the contract states that they agreed gender roles were clearly established in the Bible (GA Employment Contract, 2013).
10 According to the chart, the Christian perspective on sociology was "traditional family, church, state," while the Islamic perspective was "polygamy, mosque, Islamic state."
11 According to the chart, the Christian perspective on history was "creation, fall, redemption," while the Islamic perspective was "historical determinism (Jihad)."
12 See Chapter 2.

References

Associated Press. (2014, November 22). Texas approves disputed history texts for schools. *The New York Times*. Retrieved from www.nytimes.com/2014/11/23/us/texas-approves-disputed-history-texts-for-schools.html?_r=1
Blosser, A. H. (2017). Considerations for addressing diversity in Christian Schools. In D. B. Hiatt-Michael (Ed.), *Family and community engagement in faith-based schools* (pp. 33–55). Charlotte, NC: Information Age Publishing, Inc.
Blosser, J. (2012). Beyond moral development: Re-theorizing ethical practices in service learning. *Journal for Cultural and Religious Theory*, 12(2), 196–214.
Bowles, S., & Gintis, H. (1976). *Schooling in capitalist America*. New York, NY: Basic Books.
Brundin, J. (2014, October 4). After protests over history curriculum, school board tries to compromise. *National Public Radio*. Podcast retrieved from www.npr.org/2014/10/03/353327302/school-board-wants-civil-disorder-deemphasized-students-walk-out
College Board. (2013). *AP Biology: Course and exam description*. Retrieved from http://media.collegeboard.com/digitalServices/pdf/ap/ap-biology-course-and-exam-description.pdf
Diangelo, R. (2018). *White fragility: Why it's so hard for white people to talk about racism*. Boston, MA: Beacon Press.
Eby, J. W. (1998). *Why service learning is bad*. Retrieved from www.google.com/url?sa=t&rct=j&q=&esrc=s&source=web&cd=1&ved=0CCAQFjAA

Emerson, M. O., & Smith, C. (2000). *Divided by faith: Evangelical religion and the problem of race in America*. New York, NY: Oxford UP.

Esposito, J. (2011). Negotiating the gaze and learning the hidden curriculum: A critical race analysis of the embodiment of female students of color at a predominantly white institution. *Journal for Critical Educational Policy Studies*, 9(2), 143–164.

Francis, P., & Longhurst, M. (2014, July 23). How LGBT students are changing Christian colleges. *The Atlantic*. Retrieved from www.theatlantic.com/education/archive/2014/07/gordon-college-the-new-frontier-of-gay-rights/374861/

Gilmore, M. J., & Murphy, J. (1991). Understanding classroom environments: An organizational sensemaking approach. *Educational Administration Quarterly*, 27(3), 392–429.

Gutmann, A. (1987). *Democratic education*. Princeton, NJ: Princeton UP.

Hatt-Echeverria, B., & Jo, J. (2005). Understanding the "new" racism through an urban charter school. *Educational Foundations*, 35, 51–65.

Isensee, L. (2014, November 21). Texas hits the books. *National Public Radio*. Podcast retrieved from www.npr.org/blogs/ed/2014/11/21/365686593/texas-hits-the-books

Jay, M. (2003). Critical race theory, multicultural education, and the hidden curriculum of hegemony. *Multicultural Perspectives*, 5(4), 3–9.

Kunzman, R. (2015). Talking with students who already know the answer: Navigating ethical certainty in democratic dialogue. In J. H. James, S. Schweber, R. Kunzman, K. C. Barton, & K. Logan (Eds.), *Religion in the classroom: Dilemmas for democratic education* (pp. 79–89). New York, NY: Routledge.

Lewis, A. E. (2001). There is no 'race' in the schoolyard: Color-blind ideology in an (almost) all-white school. *American Educational Research Journal*, 38(4), 781–811.

Mehta, H. (2014, September 27). JeffCo school board (in Colorado) wants to revise the A.P. U.S. History curriculum . . . with the help of Christians. *Patheos*. Retrieved from www.patheos.com/blogs/friendlyatheist/2014/09/27/jeffco-school-board-in-colorado-wants-to-revise-the-ap-u-s-history-curriculum-with-the-help-of-christians/

Miller, B. (2018, May 6). White evangelicals are the most fragile of all white people. *Huffington Post*. Retrieved from www.huffingtonpost.com/entry/opinion-miller-white-fragility_us_5aef28ece4b0c4f19323b132

Morris, E. (2006). *An unexpected minority: White kids in an urban school*. New Brunswick, NJ, Rutgers UP.

Nelson, L. (2014, October 17). How AP US history classes became the new culture war battleground. *Vox*. Retrieved from www.vox.com/2014/10/17/6988037/how-ap-history-became-the-most-controversial-class-in-us-high-schools

PBS. (2014, October 2). AP history class standards spark fight over patriotism and censorship. Podcast retrieved from www.pbs.org/newshour/bb/ap-history-class-standards-spark-fight-patriotism-censorship/

Peshkin, A. (1986). *God's choice: The total world of a fundamentalist Christian school*. Chicago, IL: University of Chicago Press.

Phillippo, K., Brown, E. L., & Blosser, A. (2018). Making sense of student-teacher relationships: Teacher educator and candidate engagement with the relational practices of teaching. *Action in Teacher Education*, 40(2), 169–185.

Schweber, S., & Irwin, R. (2003). "Especially special": Learning about Jews in a fundamentalist Christian school. *Teachers College Record, 105*(9), 1693–1719.

Slimbach, R. (2000). First, do no harm: Short-term missions at the dawn of a new millennium. *Evangelical Missions Quarterly, 36*(10), 428–441.

Summit Ministries. (2018). *Understanding the Times bible curriculum.* Retrieved from www.summit.org/curriculum/understanding-the-times-home-school/

Wagner, M. B. (1990). *God's schools: Choice and compromise in American society.* New Brunswick, NJ: Rutgers University Press.

Wagner, M. B. (1997). Generic conservative Christianity: The demise of denominationalism in Christian schools. *Journal for the Scientific Study of Religion, 36*(1), 13–24.

Weick, K. E. (1995). *Sensemaking in organizations.* Thousand Oaks, CA: Sage Publications.

Yancey, G. (2006). *Beyond racial gridlock: Embracing mutual responsibility.* Downers Grove, IL: InterVarsity Press.

Note: I exclude references that might in any way compromise the identity of the school.

6 Lessons From Grace Academy

Public and private schools alike are making sense of diversity. No school can turn a blind eye to the diversity in their midst. Neither can teacher-educators and school administrators ignore the influence of school context on student experiences. Further, the public simply must consider who education is for and what its purpose is, and decide if publicly funded voucher programs work toward those ends.

Grace Academy's story, a story of faith, diversity, and education, therefore, has a lot to teach us. It is the story of how an "outside" idea—diversity—got taken up by a school. It reveals the complexity of addressing diversity in a context that is largely wary of diversity, at least in its typical secular usage. Doing diversity at Grace Academy was framed by two opposing ideologies: conservative Christianity and secularism (Blosser, 2017). The question for school stakeholders became how to address what they considered to be an essentially secular value (diversity) in a way that didn't require them to compromise their conservative Christian values or disrupt their existing school culture (Blosser, 2017). Further, it required a choice between "tradition" and "transformation" (Shange & Slaughter-Defoe, 2011, p. 51), but that choice wasn't straightforward. Stakeholders' sensemaking about diversity at GA revealed desires to preserve the status quo (namely, the Christian identity and ethos of the school) *and* recognition of the need for change. But some school stakeholders wanted the perception of transformation without uprooting tradition. Because these desires coexisted, administrators struggled to craft a diversity initiative that encouraged change and yet did not require faculty and staff to change their current practices. Further, embedded in the opposition between conservative Christianity and secularism, tradition, and transformation were several tensions complicating GA's diversity efforts.

The most prominent tension was created by faculty, staff, and administrators' theologically grounded belief in colorblindness and their desire to both see more color in GA's demographics and educate students about diversity. This tension manifested as school administrators claimed that they employed colorblind, meritocratic recruitment practices, yet their implicit racial bias caused them to apply "fit" differently to black students and teachers. They also didn't want to adopt what they deemed to be secular ways of becoming more diverse, such as setting quotas, which require institutions to pay attention to race in hiring and admissions processes. Yet, in many ways, they did just that by quantifying the maximum percentage of black football players they would accept. Moreover, the school wanted to create an environment where students would learn to celebrate their differences, but they wanted to do so without drawing attention to differences in the curricula or programming. As a result, students primarily learned about diversity implicitly through activities designed to make them better Christians. Because these efforts weren't intentional and served other purposes, students were learning disparate lessons about diversity. Meanwhile, black students and parents, the primary population the school was trying to recruit and retain, claimed that more color-attuned practices like Culturally Relevant Pedagogy and explicit discussions of race would improve their schooling experiences.

The school administration's narrow conservative Christian conception of diversity was also in tension with the students' more inclusive conceptions of diversity. This tension was revealed in students' identification of UTT and the Policy for Biblical Living as important sites of diversity learning, despite the fact that religious difference and sexual orientation were not identified as facets of identity in the school's diversity statement. Not only were students' conceptions of diversity more inclusive than the administration's but also some students held different attitudes than the administration about the school's diversity practices and the messages imparted therein, which at times left students reluctant to share their opinions with their peers and teachers, and led them to take their education into their own hands.

Finally, there was the overarching tension created from stakeholders' desires to accommodate the pressures of secular culture versus the conservative Christian theological mandates to reject them. This tension was implicit in the school's conservative Christian framing of diversity, but it became explicit in the wide variation in faculty, staff, and administrators' sensemaking about the motivations for addressing diversity. The tension also became apparent in AP Biology where teachers taught the theory of evolution, knowledge students needed to pass the AP Biology exam, but also taught why the theory was flawed from a conservative Christian Creationist perspective.

GA's diversity efforts were simultaneously defined and subverted by its effort to make students into strong conservative Christians. Its story demonstrates that sensemaking about diversity in schools is largely shaped by organizational context. Thus, diversity does not mean the same thing, nor can it be addressed the same way in all schools (Blosser, 2017). And organizational forces can undercut a school's best efforts to address diversity.

The final pages of this book demonstrate the lessons learned from GA's story, lessons of white fragility and curated diversity, lessons about the impact of teachers' religious identities, lessons informing the school voucher debate, and lessons about the morality and existence of Christian schools. The chapter concludes with a look at GA today and what they've done to address diversity in the few years since I was there.

White Fragility and Curated Diversity

Grace Academy's story adds to contemporary conversations about white fragility and curated diversity. The term "white fragility" became popularized by Robin Diangelo (2018) in her New York Times bestselling book, *White Fragility: Why It's So Hard for White People to Talk about Racism*. DiAngelo (2018) explains how white fragility refers to the reluctance, anxiety, discomfort, defensiveness, guilt, fear, etc., that white people experience when asked to talk about race, acknowledge their membership in a racial group, or admit the advantages that their race affords them in the US.

Brandi Miller (2018) specifically addresses the fragility of white evangelicals. In her article, "White Evangelicals Are the Most Fragile of All White People," Miller (2018) described her experience of attending a missions conference facilitated by a group of mostly white evangelicals. One night of the conference focused on "black styles of worship and preaching," and included a preacher "exhort[ing] the thousands present to repent of the ways that evangelicalism is in bed with white supremacy." Miller (2018) explains how the black participants felt heard and cared about because their cultural practices and experiences were affirmed. Shortly after that evening, however, some of the white attendees demonstrated white fragility as they began to suggest that "calling out white racism was persecution or created disunity in the body of Christ" (Miller, 2018). Miller's experience and her assertion that white evangelicals saw the admonition of white racism as a divisive act resonated with my research at GA. The preaching that night that Miller describes is akin to using Culturally Relevant Pedagogy, something GA resisted because it could create disunity. Miller (2018) goes on to explain the defensive posture white Christians assume when the impact of their whiteness is questioned because they see themselves as moral people who have been saved by Jesus. Any assertion that they are complicit with racist structures because of the God-given color of their skin is an affront to their faith (Miller, 2018).

I interpreted a lot of white fragility in GA's school community. The school valued Christian identity formation above all else and used the language of unity in Christ to frame all matters of diversity. Seeded in that language of unity was a fear of dividing their school community by acknowledging and affirming students' individual differences. It was out of a fearful grip on "unity" that GA took a defensive posture around certain issues, such as Mrs. Griffin. This is also why the school taught students how to defend their faith at all costs. Miller (2018) continues to explain the implications of white fragility—namely, the continued marginalization and silencing of people of color, and the lack of safe spaces for people of color to share their experiences. Ultimately, she (2018) claims that white evangelicals are choosing to react defensively about race and that instead they need to allow and engage in conversations about race and listen to and empathize with people of color, even if such conversations and space create discomfort for them. It is clear that GA's black students and parents desired such conversations. It is likely that the school's white stakeholders could learn a great deal about the oneness of Christ's body if they participated in conversations that could help them better empathize with how other parts of the one body experience the world.

GA, like many other private and public schools, was "curating diversity" (Hannah-Jones, 2017, as cited in Douglas, 2017). Hannah-Jones uses this term to describe how white communities create school environments to reflect the diversity they desire (as cited in Douglas, 2017). That is, the school environments they seek are still predominantly white, but they want enough black/brown students to make the white people feel as though their kids' schools are diverse. Hannah-Jones says that for white communities, the desired percentage of black/brown students is around 10%–15%, but once that percentage climbs over 20%, white community members begin to believe the school is too black and start perceiving the percentage of black/brown students to be greater than it is (as cited Douglas, 2017). She maintains that when the public school to which white families are zoned is too black, white families start demanding choice or simply move to another school district (as cited in Douglas, 2017). Hannah-Jones also points out how white families desire middle-class families of color in their kids' schools, but not poor students of color (as cited in Douglas, 2017). If Hannah-Jones's assertion about poor students of color is correct, and I suspect it is, then predominantly white private schools that increasingly accept low-income students of color via voucher programs may begin to face opposition from their tuition-paying white families (as cited Douglas, 2017).

Grace Academy curated diversity as a form of identity protection. It wanted students of color, but only certain kinds of black students (e.g., athletes, Christians, black students from two-parent households)—"good kids." Bringing in athletes of color, in particular, was okay from the perspective of some white GA students because they could secure the school state titles and fit with existing stereotypes of blackness and athleticism. But the teams still needed to be half white to keep parents happy. Likewise, GA wanted black teachers, but only black teachers who fit the norms of the school. GA was trying to craft a population that both kept the dominant group and ideology in power, and led to the school having a good reputation for being diverse.

Sadly, schools aren't the only US institutions that are curating diversity. President Trump's border wall and immigration policies are just the latest attempts in a long line of US laws and policies aimed to distinguish good immigrants from bad immigrants. President Trump also ensured that our institutions of higher education have a harder time seeking diverse students when he eliminated the Obama-era Affirmative Action guidelines that had urged universities to consider race in their admissions processes and extoled the benefits of having diverse classmates (Green, Apuzzo, & Benner, 2018). White evangelicals have tended to support such policies (Wong, 2018). The more a school's policies and practices distinguish good from bad diversity, the more students will learn the value of exclusion through the school's hidden curriculum and organizational culture. Such learning will produce more people who support exclusionary policies, such as border walls, voter restrictions, travel bans, and the like.

Educators' Religious Identities

Grace Academy's story indicates the potential significance of religious beliefs on educators' practice. At GA, religious ideology was the most dominant factor shaping educators' sensemaking about diversity. It influenced buy-in (or not) of the school's diversity initiative, the nature and implementation of the school's diversity policies and practices, and teachers' choices of course content. Conservative Christian ideology shaped the facets of identity that were deemed legitimate, the organizational commitment to colorblindness, and teachers' choices to not practice culturally relevant pedagogy.

GA's story, then, teaches us that religious beliefs influence the environment teachers create, as well as their actions in the classroom. While this is expected at religious schools like GA, one can't presume that public school teachers are immune to the influence of their religious beliefs. Humans simply aren't that good at compartmentalizing their beliefs from their work. And researchers tend to agree. Marshall (2009) found that pre-service teachers used spiritual constructs for thinking about teaching. And White (2010) found in a collective case study she conducted that teachers' religious beliefs shaped their teaching in five ways: their reasons for becoming teachers, their approach to student/teacher relationships, their methods of classroom management and discipline, their views of various groups of people and their recognition of inequitable practices, and how they engaged religion and religious content in the classroom. Both White (2009, 2010) and Marshall (2009) then argue that teacher preparation programs need to encourage teachers to consider how their own religious identities impact their attitudes and practices in the classroom. I agree, especially given that US teachers, as a subset of the population, are more likely than other Americans to go to church, pray daily, and "[feel] extremely close to God" (Slater, 2008).

Vouchers

Grace's story informs the current policy debates about school vouchers. Neither the school's admissions practices based on "fit" nor their conservative Christian framing of subject matter (like teaching creationism over evolution) further the secular public interest. But Grace Academy didn't want to produce secular citizens. They wanted to produce Christian citizens who would keep their faith and spread the gospel in a secular world.

Both Christian schools and the wider public, then, have reasons to be leery of voucher programs. The secular public should be concerned that public dollars are being used to support private schools that are not being held publicly accountable for what they teach or their admissions practices. These schools are not legally required to teach students the skills and values necessary to be good citizens, though some do. Nor are they prohibited from discriminating against some groups of students, though not all do. The findings discussed in this book should prompt researchers, policy makers, private school stakeholders, and the wider public to consider developing accountability measures for voucher-accepting private schools and the possible implications if they do.

Christian schools should also be wary of voucher programs. By accepting public money, Christian schools find themselves in the paradoxical position of ideologically rejecting secular culture even as they rely on its money. By accepting public monies, Christian schools run the risk of having to compromise their missions, because if a school becomes financially dependent on government voucher dollars, then it would be essentially relinquishing control to the government. After all, the Bible—their guidebook—says, "Where your treasure is, your heart will be also" (Matthew 6:21). The story of GA likely rings true for other conservative Christian school leaders. The tensions such schools face between their theology and the secular world will only increase as their dependence on secular tax dollars increases.

The Morality and Existence of Christian Schools

Grace Academy's story raises questions about Christian schools' morality and right to exist. In a provocative interview in the *Atlantic*, Hannah-Jones (2017) answers the question, "Are private schools immoral?" (as cited in Douglas, 2017). She asserts that private schools are part of the problem of school segregation and equality in the US, and that to integrate schools and create equal schooling for all children, we would have to abolish private schools (Douglas, 2017). This question is similar to the one Peshkin (1986) addressed in the final pages of his ethnography, which is whether or not Christian schools should be allowed to exist. He ultimately came to a different conclusion and rationalized that they should be allowed to exist unless there is definitive evidence that they are dangerous to society:

> The *potential* for abuse, however, does not establish the state's compelling interest to abolish either the political or the educational arms of absolutist Christian groups. To be sure, they may indeed become a "clear and present danger" to our open society, but until that time has been judged to exist, we must abide by the paradoxes Madison's liberty produces and remain mindful of liberty's effects. Meanwhile their institutions must not be slandered, their leaders must not be vilified, their students and teachers must not be taken to task for what they *may* do. Their right to thrive is inviolable, at least until they overstep the line between safe and unsafe—an extraordinarily difficult issue to decide—and thereby signal that it is time for intolerance to replace tolerance. Tolerance, after all, is only a limited good.
>
> (p. 299)

Peshkin's rationale in many ways still works if tolerance is what we value as a society. I would take his argument a step further and suggest that today, the very question Peshkin set out to answer has changed. The existence of Christian schools is not the issue. The issue is the public funding of them and whether we as a society are going to continue to privilege the free exercise of religion over the marginalization of people of color and LGBTQ individuals. Because that's what happening when we publicly fund religious schools where those things are occurring. Therefore, the US public should ask, "What are the values and practices we are demanding from schools when they accept public dollars?"

Peshkin (1986) further argued that the mere existence of conservative Christian schools "creates a paradox of pluralism in the United States" (p. 298). As he (1986) explains, Christian schools depend on Americans' value of pluralism for their survival, but pluralism isn't a value they are willing to instill in their students. Rather, Christian school students are taught that other people's beliefs are wrong and to react defensively to disagreements with their theology. Peshkin (1986) contended that such a paradox was indicative of our country's "ideological health" (p. 298). As he (1986) put it about Bethany Baptist Academy, "From the perspective of the pluralist America that I value I see that the more successful the Bethanys of America are, the less successful will be the ideal of pluralism which assures their survival" (295). Again, the rub is how to agree upon the purpose and responsibilities of schools and whether to hold schools accountable for meeting those ends, an agreement that is becoming ever more complicated and significant in an age of school choice.

Grace Academy Today

What did GA do in response to your findings? Where is GA today? These are the questions I get whenever I present the findings from this study.

During the original study, I regularly met with Dr. Smith to share my findings and verify and refine my analysis. I also, per his request, prepared a list of practical recommendations that I shared with him in one of our final interactions. A few years later, I used the recommendations I shared with him and some of the study's findings to develop a list of considerations for Christian schools wanting to address diversity. I published these considerations in a book on faith-based schools (see Blosser, 2017). As that book chapter was my first publication on this study of GA and was written with Christian school leaders in mind as the intended audience, I sent it to Dr. Smith. Dr. Smith called me shortly after reading the publication to share his reaction to it. He reacted positively to the chapter and felt my depiction of the school to be fair. But he was also eager to tell me about what GA has done to address diversity since I was last there several years ago. This conversation, coupled with the questions I repeatedly got about GA's response to my findings, prompted me to seek Institutional Review Board (IRB) approval for a formal follow-up interview with Dr. Smith, which I conducted in the summer of 2018.

It had been several years since I last walked through GA's doors, but it was as if no time had passed. Many of the same women, my gatekeepers into the world of GA, were still working in the front office, and we picked up right where we left off. They warmly asked me about my family, and I asked about theirs. I was reminded of just how welcoming this community was to me. My first reaction was that nothing had changed. But my perception was altered when I stepped into Dr. Smith's office. I sensed that he had changed. Piled on his desk were well-respected books about how to address diversity and facilitate challenging conversations about race. Further, it became clear in our conversation that he had been reading, learning, and thinking about these issues. Our conversation was honest, raw, and gritty in a way our conversations hadn't been a few years ago. Dr. Smith seemed more aware of the challenges he was facing in "doing diversity." There was very little defensiveness and lots of concessions as we reviewed my findings and again discussed GA's challenges for the future.

From my perspective as both an outsider and as someone intimately familiar with the challenges he was facing, it appeared that GA in general and Dr. Smith, in particular, had made progress in addressing diversity. Most notably, 15% of GA's student population were racial/ethnic minorities, the school hired another black teacher, and GA changed its admissions policies to be more inclusive. In addition, faculty and staff attended some professional development on diversity. Dr. Smith and two other administrators attended a ten-week program on multiethnic conversations, and the four principals, as well as many other staff members, had attended a two-day diversity training program. Dr. Smith had also been inviting women and speakers of color to speak at chapel and began encouraging his staff and administrators to rethink their color-blind perspectives.

Demographic Changes

The most significant indicator of progress toward GA's diversity goals was that its minority student population increased from 9% to 15% of the student body. Dr. Smith explained that this growth was largely due to the state's new voucher program and GA's acceptance of voucher students. When I was at Grace several years ago, the state's voucher program had not yet been implemented (even though there was a large political push for it), so I didn't directly ask about school vouchers in my interviews with stakeholders. I also didn't realize at the time just how much GA's story would inform that debate. But I did note in my analytic memos how stakeholders hoped the state's proposed voucher program would increase the diversity of the school. Dr. Smith had been among those pushing for the program as he, and many others in GA's community, were aware that the proposed program was designed to offer choice to low-income families. Since income level and race were largely correlated in the state, the program could help increase two important forms of diversity at GA. In my original study, I heard statements such as

> if this voucher program goes through, that means we're going to be able to attract a lot more families in the lower economic category, which likely will mean more diversity.
> (Dr. Smith, the head of school)

> With this new voucher passing, I'm hoping that that will help some lower income families and give us some more diversity.
> (Mrs. Marshall, a parent)

> To me, if Grace can affect one kid like that from whatever background they're from, if you can bring them in on a scholarship or a voucher grant or whatever you want to call it and then you can spit them out on the other end with some morals and some values and some ethics and that sort of thing, then that's money well spent.
> (Mr. Fuller, a parent)

Notwithstanding the embedded assumption of Mr. Fuller's comment— that voucher students lack morals and values— I had noted to myself back then how vouchers were one way GA could become more diverse without requiring that the school radically change its recruitment and retention practices. The fact that vouchers can help conservative Christian schools become more diverse without having to change any of their policies, practices, or curricula makes them very alluring to these schools. Voucher students are also still a selective group, because they tend to come from families who 1) are involved enough in their children's education to pursue a voucher and go through the lengthy process of applying for private schools and 2) can provide transportation. This makes it quite possible that minority students who get vouchers are more likely to "fit" GA's expectations for desirable minority students. Therefore, when I had the opportunity to conduct a follow-up interview with Dr. Smith, knowing the state's voucher program was now in place, I had to ask about its impact on GA.

The state's voucher program awards families below a certain income threshold a voucher for their child to attend private school. Dr. Smith credited the voucher program as the main reason GA's percentage of minority students had increased. Additionally, he claimed that the voucher program had drastically increased the socioeconomic diversity of the school, and Dr. Smith boasted that a recent school consultant visited GA and claimed it to be the "most socioeconomically diverse school he has ever worked with." Dr. Smith estimated that GA had 50 students who attended GA on vouchers. These students, he claimed, came from "good solid families." Assumptions about what constituted "good" families aside, Dr. Smith's comment implied that GA still got to be selective about who they admitted.

I asked what percentage of his voucher students were athletes because I had shared with him my finding that students tended to associate minority students with athletics. He responded, "I can probably count on one hand how many are athletes." I also asked Dr. Smith if he fears government regulation because they accepted vouchers. He said he did and explained that many independent schools choose not to accept vouchers for fear of having to compromise their missions. He also explained that GA would now have to cap the number of voucher students it accepted because once schools accepted a certain threshold of voucher dollars, which GA was close to meeting, schools became more regulated.[1] While he had no doubt that GA would pass any measure of accountability for schools accepting that much funding, he didn't want the increased regulation.

That said, Dr. Smith said he would like to see greater accountability in the state's voucher program because there was hardly any. This opinion surprised me knowing how politically conservative Dr. Smith tended to lean and that conservatives tended to resist government regulation of private enterprise. But according to Dr. Smith, vouchers can be used at schools that aren't accredited and many are being used at such schools. I verified the accuracy of Dr. Smith's statement through some research into the state's regulation of vouchers.[2] He explained that the state's voucher program comes with little regulation compared to other voucher programs, and while independent schools value autonomy, there needed to be a few more regulations. Limiting the eligible schools to accredited schools would be his solution.

Despite such loose restrictions with the state's voucher program, Dr. Smith complained that he did have to report test scores for his voucher students as an indication of their progress. The state, however, did not accept scores from the standardized test GA usually administered. So during the week when GA students participated in GA's chosen standardized test, voucher students had to be pulled out and administered a different test. Such a practice runs the risk of identifying and/or marginalizing students who attend schools on vouchers, which is a problem that has been documented elsewhere (Beabout & Cambre, 2013). Future studies should be conducted on the integration and potential marginalization of voucher students in private schools.

After my interview with Dr. Smith, I reached out to him for the racial/ethnic breakdown of his voucher students. Initially, GA didn't have such a breakdown, but at Dr. Smith's request, they gathered the data for me and the school to have. The data revealed that GA actually enrolled over 60 voucher students, 58.7% of whom are white. When they broke down the data further, it revealed that 21% of the students identified as black, with the next most frequent identification as "unknown" (8%). No other racial/ethnic category had more than two students enrolled. Interestingly, GA also provided the racial/ethnic breakdown of students attending the school on the state's grant for students with disabilities, which is a large grant given to families who have children with special needs so they can send their children to private school. The breakdown was stark. Ninety percent of the approximately 20 students attending GA with that grant identified as white. These racial breakdowns differ from the state's percentages of students receiving these grants. While I was unable to locate the race/ethnicity demographics of disabilities grant recipients in the state, only 40% of the students receiving vouchers in the state are white, while 36% are black and 9% are Latino.[3] GA's voucher students are proportionately whiter and less black than the state's voucher recipients as whole, but only slightly whiter and less black than Cedar Ridge's population. The fact that around 40% of GA's voucher students are nonwhite suggests that the voucher program is helping GA's student population to become more racially and ethnically diverse. The program is certainly making the school more socioeconomically diverse.

Enrollment Agreement Changes

Aside from demographics, another major change at GA was that they altered the document that parents have to sign when they agree to enroll their child at GA. The new enrollment agreement was "a little bit broader," to use Dr. Smith's words, and it gave parents the agency to enroll their children at GA, instead of giving the school the agency to decide upfront that a student or family's lifestyle won't fit. "Why would you deny a child coming in?" Dr. Smith asked. Dr. Smith explained how the new enrollment agreement was largely developed in response to the situation I described with the gay student and all of the negative attention Christian schools have received in the press concerning LGBTQ families. He developed an official statement on gender, sexuality, and marriage outlining GA's beliefs about these things. In it, the school was able to establish their beliefs that[4]

1. God "immutably" creates biological sex as male or female, which are "complementary" by design. To refuse one's biological sex is to also refuse the "image of God," and thereby no one should try to change their God-given biological sex.
2. Marriage is scripturally defined as the union between a man and woman. Sexual relations should occur only between married men and women, and no intimate acts should occur outside of and/or prior to marriage.
3. All acts of "sexual immorality," like utilizing pornography, sexual acts with members of the same sex, fornication, adultery, etc., are forms of sin. And because God created men and women to be sexually "complementary," people should combat any attractions to and/or refrain from engaging in sexual acts with members of the same sex.
4. Because they are Christian role models to students, GA staff must accept and follow the doctrines and behaviors in this statement.
5. God will forgive and redeem anyone who forsakes their sins.
6. Scripture demands that we treat others with respect and kindness, so harassment or hate speech directed at any student should be renounced (GA Enrollment Agreement, 2018).

GA also added to their Statement of Faith a declaration about when life begins (at conception) and their "calling" to defend life at all stages. In signing the enrollment agreement, parents agree that they have read and support those statements, as well as GA's statements of faith, mission, and philosophy. GA's diversity statement also appeared in GA's enrollment agreement (2018). Further, there was a clause added to the agreement that said parents understand that GA will teach these values and principles. As Dr. Smith explained it to me, that clause was important because it established to families, "This is who we are. If you want that and support that teaching in your home, then you're welcome." He said that adding that statement and language to the contract wasn't so harsh as to say that parents couldn't enroll their student at GA if they (the parents) or the (student) were gay, but it did let them know what was believed and taught at the school. He said it had led to a lot of "honest dialogues" with people considering GA. He even recounted a conversation he had with two moms who weren't reportedly concerned about the conservative environment but were concerned about their child being included and invited to sleepovers with other GA kids. Dr. Smith went on to explain how the statement and the enrollment agreement "put[s] the decision back on the parent," instead of the school, to decide if the environment and teaching was a right fit. "You know what you're signing up for," he said. And this shift in perspective had apparently helped with retention. According to Dr. Smith, ACSI was apparently so impressed with GA's adoption of the statement and the careful rewording of its enrollment agreement that it shared it with other member schools to use as a model.

So I directly asked Dr. Smith if he would still counsel a gay student to withdraw. He explained, "We have dealt with a couple of gay parents and kids that are grappling with sexuality issues and identity, those types of things. So we don't kick them out." He admitted that a few of GA's graduates have come out after they graduated and stressed to me that it was the practice of acting on or celebrating same-sex attractions that were the problematic behaviors in their view. But he also acknowledged that GA probably wouldn't be the "ideal environment" and that life at the school would likely be "harder than it needs to be" for a student or family who disagrees with GA's statements on gender, sexuality, and marriage because the teaching at GA is going to reflect its stance. He said that the school community changed in that it no longer viewed practicing homosexuality as "the number one sin of all sins." Rather, the GA community recognized that, "in the grand scheme of sin, this is one of them. We are all born thieves and liars and cheaters and whatever." That said, the enrollment agreement still included a clause that the school reserves the right to discipline a student (which includes dismissing a student) if the students engages in behavior "inconsistent" with biblical living as "prescribed" by GA's sponsoring church, though that clause did not specifically mention any sexual practices.

Dr. Smith realized that many parents nowadays come from a "totally different value system." He added, "We understand who we serve, and it's a much broader Christian culture and neutral evangelical environment. You do not have to be a Protestant or professing Christian to attend the school," he proclaimed. Admittedly, that was the case several years ago as well, but to hear him say that surprised me. He reiterated, "You just need to understand the environment you're coming into." And GA's new enrollment agreement reflected that sentiment in that it stated that GA would consider admitting students from families who, despite their religious affiliation or beliefs, were willing to support GA's positions, allowing their children to be educated according to those positions. GA was becoming more accommodating and, perhaps, even assimilating to secular culture.

Changes in Thinking About Colorblindness

Dr. Smith's thinking about colorblindness had also changed. In one of our conversations several years ago, Dr. Smith told me how he liked the term "colorblind" to describe the school community. But years later, he appeared to understand the marginalizing impact of colorblind practices. And he was trying to get faculty and staff to understand that impact as well. But he added that he believed his faculty and staff's use of the term was a "well-intentioned," albeit "naïve," way for them to say, "We don't discriminate. [. . .] We love all these kids like they're our own kids no matter if they're white or brown, or no matter what their background." He instructed his staff to stop using the term, but abandoning a colorblind curriculum still seemed to be a work in progress. Dr. Smith said the school was still opposed to celebrating Cinco de Mayo, Dr. Martin Luther King Day, or Black History Month, but he wanted something more meaningful for the curriculum. He implied that while thinking around colorblindness was evolving, the school didn't practice some of the more common, or from their perspective, "secular" ways of honoring different cultures in school. As we talked more about it, he explained how he thought there was a better way to celebrate differences, and he had solicited the guidance of an African American GA parent who specialized in racial reconciliation to help figure out what Culturally Relevant Pedagogy in a Christian context might look like.

Persistent Challenges

All of these strides aside, Dr. Smith wished he had more progress to report concerning GA's diversity efforts: "I had hoped we would be a little further along. I'm very pleased where we are with our student body. I'm pleased that the administrative team sees the necessity of really working harder to have a more balanced faculty and staff." He later admitted, "I think if we had the right diversity coordinator that probably we could have been further along." He explained that diversity work was not Coach Wade's specialty; rather, it was coaching. But he still saw his two top priorities as diversifying the staff (and finding the "right" diverse staff) and building the school's cultural intelligence.

We also revisited Mrs. Griffin, and I wondered if hindsight had changed his perspective on how things ended with her. For the most part, Dr. Smith's perspective on the situation appeared to remain the same. Dr. Smith explained that she visited the school several times a year, and he was thankful that things ended so well with her. He reiterated to me that it was her academic instruction that caused her to be dismissed, not her race, though he did admit that she had a "strong agenda" and explained how such an agenda "is never gonna fit" at GA. He also said two things I hadn't heard him say about her before. First, he thought he could have helped her assimilate or better fit into GA's culture had her agenda been her only stumbling block. But her agenda, coupled with the deficiencies in her academic instruction, provided enough grounds to dismiss her. Second, he conceded that he should have been "more hands on" as she acclimated and added that the kind of culturally relevant instruction she provided "would have been a better fit perhaps, maybe in high school." He was hopeful that the new African American teacher he'd hired would have a different outcome. He explained how he had to work really hard to recruit her. Apparently, she came with great recommendations from another predominantly white Christian school in the South, so we discussed how she might have a better sense of what to expect from the culture of GA.

Dr. Smith also described the isolation he felt in doing diversity work at GA:

> I wish I wasn't the only one carrying this flag. And that's the way it feels at times [. . .] This is my own internal urgency. So there's no internal or external pressure [asking], "Why aren't you doing this?" "Why isn't it better?" I have those voices.

He explained that while he had made GA's diversity initiative a priority, other administrators had not, which had at times created conflict between them and led to some "tough conversations" about why addressing diversity is important and, in particular, why GA needed to diversify its staff. And because he had been doing this work alone and had to garner buy-in, he explained how, "other things are being impacted as a result. I'm not able to do the other things efficiently because I'm spending so much time navigating and having those discussions. It's frustrating." He wanted some help in leading the school's diversity initiative so that he could focus on other priorities. He told me he had begun to chip away at the school culture and had been able to "push a little bit harder," as he gradually gained more capital in the school community. He still, however, felt like the guy from up North who approached diversity from an entirely different context. "I'm still a Yankee," he lamented and then added, "I realize the diversity I came from."

Resistant parents, in particular, remained a challenge, he asserted. He explained that a huge obstacle in GA's community was that their current demographics were "comfortable" for many GA's families. But it became clear that the parents to which he was referring were white families: "We're not getting challenges from the African American families, or Latino, or Asian." He attributed white families' comfort not only to the predominantly white demographic but also to the environment. He said his response to such claims from parents was, "Yeah, but it's (GA's demographics) not representative of our city. We're not in charge of trying to fix the whole world. But we're here to address these issues that are ours, and so I take ownership of that."

The Future

I asked Dr. Smith how he would know when he had been successful in implementing GA's diversity initiative. He responded that his goal for GA was to have a 20% racial/ethnic minority student population and a more diverse staff because he learned in his ten-week diversity training that an organization is considered "multiethnic" when 20% of its population identified as racial/ethnic minorities. I found it interesting that Dr. Smith quantified a desired percentage of diverse students given his dislike of targets and quotas, but he quickly explained to me that he would never actually set a quota of needing to achieve a certain percentage by a certain date. He and I also discussed what meeting that 20% might mean for GA. I shared with him Hannah-Jones's (2017) assertion that once a white school community reaches 20% minority students, white families start exaggerating the percentage of diverse students and get uncomfortable (as cited in Douglas, 2017). Dr. Smith said he was ready to face those objections. The "much stronger goal," he stated, "is staff . . . Because the progress isn't being made on the staffing side. Period."

Dr. Smith's diversity training also informed one of his other aspirations. He learned how he wanted to reframe the rhetoric around diversity in the school so that addressing diversity becomes a "discipleship issue" and not a diversity issue. Reframing GA's diversity initiative in this way would help him gain buy-in because it would further "desecularize" the initiative. It would help him show faculty and staff how the diversity work he wanted to accomplish would further the primary organizational goal—making strong Christians. Instead of going alone against the culture, he could ride the current.

He also repeatedly mentioned that he wanted more discussions about diversity with students, staff, and parents. He passionately exclaimed, "We are not doing enough. [. . .] It's having those tough conversations, fierce conversations, being very honest with parents, making it part of our language." This exclamation is a far cry from the faculty meeting I observed in which Dr. Smith hesitantly introduced the diversity statement by making light of the issue and offering no space to discuss it (observation, November 4, 2013). Clearly, he had become more willing to have tough conversations. Mainly, though, Dr. Smith wanted to find the right people to help lead these changes so he could address diversity in a way that made sense for GA and didn't cause mission drift. Only time will tell, but GA has a leader committed to the hard and complex goal of prioritizing diversity in a community reluctant to transform.

Notes

1 I did not disclose the amount in order to not reveal the state in which GA is housed, but upon further research into the state's voucher program, the increased regulation once a school accepts a certain amount is a review of the school's finances.
2 Reference suppressed to not reveal the state in which GA is located.
3 Reference suppressed to not reveal the state in which GA is housed.
4 The tenets are paraphrased so that the school cannot be easily identified via an Internet search.

References

Beabout, B. R., & Cambre, B. M. (2013). Parental voucher enrollment decisions: Choice within choice in New Orleans. *Journal of School Choice*, 7(4), 560–588.

Blosser, A. H. (2017). Considerations for addressing diversity in Christian schools. In D. B. Hiatt-Michael (Ed.), *Family and community engagement in faith-based schools* (pp. 33–55). Charlotte, NC: Information Age Publishing, Inc.

Diangelo, R. (2018). *White fragility: Why it's so hard for white people to talk about racism*. Boston, MA: Beacon Press.

Douglas, D. (2017, December 14). Are private schools immoral: A conversation with Nikole Hannah-Jones about race, education, and democracy. *The Atlantic*. Retrieved from www.theatlantic.com/education/archive/2017/12/progressives-are-undermining-public-schools/548084/

Green, E., Apuzzo, M., & Benner, K. (2018, July 3). Trump officials reverse Obama's policy on affirmative action in schools. *New York Times*. Retrieved from www.nytimes.com/2018/07/03/us/politics/trump-affirmative-action-race-schools.html

Marshall, J. (2009). Describing the elephant: Preservice teachers talk about spiritual reasons for becoming a teacher. *Teacher Education Quarterly*, 36(2), 25–44.

Miller, B. (2018, May 6). White evangelicals are the most fragile of all white people. *Huffington Post*. Retrieved from www.huffingtonpost.com/entry/opinion-miller-white-fragility_us_5aef28ece4b0c4f19323b132

Peshkin, A. (1986). *God's choice: The total world of a fundamentalist Christian school*. Chicago, IL: University of Chicago Press.

Shange, S., & Slaughter-Defoe, D. T. (2011). Whither go the status quo? Independent education at the turn of the twenty-first century. In D. T. Slaughter-Defoe, H. C. Stevenson, E. G. Arrington, & D. J. Johnson (Eds.), *Black educational choice: Assessing the private and public alternatives to traditional K–12 public schools* (pp. 49–63). Santa Barbara, CA: ABC-CLIO, LLC.

Slater, R. (2008). American teachers: What values do they hold? *Education Next*, 8(1). Retrieved from http://educationnext.org/american-teachers/

White, K. (2009). Connecting religion and teacher identity: The unexplored relationship between teachers and religion in public schools. *Teaching and Teacher Education*, 25(6), 857–866.

White, K. (2010). Asking sacred questions: Understanding religion's impact on teacher belief and practice. *Religion and Education*, 37(1), 40–59.

Wong, J. (2018, June 19). This is why white evangelicals still support Trump. (It's not economic anxiety.) *The Washington Post*. Retrieved from www.washingtonpost.com/news/monkey-cage/wp/2018/06/19/white-evangelicals-still-support-donald-trump-because-theyre-more-conservative-than-other-evangelicals-this-is-why/?utm_term=.20cb1bd5e376

Note: I exclude references that might in any way compromise the identity of the school.

Final Thoughts

I am deeply concerned about the moral health of the US because hate crimes and acts of white supremacy are experiencing a resurgence, and legislative measures and literal walls are being erected to curate a society governed by conservative, white, American-born men. In such a context, it is exigent to understand how school communities, particularly conservative white school communities, think about, teach, and act upon diversity so that we can understand the theological and ideological narratives that are shaping their thinking about diverse others.

I left my follow-up interview with Dr. Smith feeling hopeful for GA's future diversity efforts because they had a committed leader who had made those efforts a priority. He was willing to learn from the school's successes and failures. But while I am hopeful for GA, I am not convinced that other Christian schools have leaders with the same sense of commitment as Dr. Smith, because as he admitted, no one else was pressuring him to work on diversity. I fear that the dominance of the resistant attitudes I encountered at GA may be indicative of the cultures of other Christian schools, but I hesitate to generalize. As Dr. Smith observed, he won't be able to move the needle alone. I hope he will be able to find the support he needs to achieve his vision. But I also hope that his and the GA community's thinking about diversity will continue to evolve to be more inclusive.

I worry that conservative Christian schools generally use their resistance to secular culture as a smoke screen for meaningfully addressing diversity. While it is unrealistic to think that school leaders would reject their resistance to secular culture, I would challenge Christian school leaders to ask what they can learn from others and what seemingly secular practices might actually have some biblical support. Personally, I believe that there is a biblical basis for recognizing diversity, rejecting white supremacy, engaging in antiracist work, and honoring the sexual orientation with which we are born. But I also know that in acknowledging my personal belief about the LGBTQ community, in particular, I will firmly secure my place as an outsider in the eyes of many conservative Christians. Regardless, as Russo, Soules, Newman, and Douglas (2018) argue, Christian schools are going to have to deal with issues of diversity in some sense because of changing social mores and legislation:

> One of the challenges for Protestant schools as they continue to evolve into the 21st century will be finding ways to balance their theological values and identities with changing social norms and helping students to negotiate the tensions that may arise, especially for more socially and theologically conservative schools. Schools will need to navigate tensions between their beliefs and doctrine with laws on discrimination based on sexual orientation and gender identity and insurance requirements for funding contraceptives.
> (p. 172)

GA already faced some of these very tensions: specifically, a student body who defined diversity more broadly then the administration.

Many prominent evangelicals have taken open public stances on diversity issues, such as immigration (e.g., Beth Moore, Ann Voskamp, Tim Keller, Max Lucado), LGBTQ rights (e.g., Tony Campolo, Jen Hatmaker, Rachel Held Evans, David Gushee), and rejecting white supremacy (e.g., Scott Arbeiter, Albert Moehler), by calling for a more inclusive Christian church and/or country. While I still disagree with some of these individuals' stances on various issues, I am encouraged that they are entering into contemporary conversations of faith and diversity instead of remaining satisfied with the status quo and/or blindly following party lines. Christian schools need to be a part of this conversation as well, especially since they are educating so many kids.

As I've argued elsewhere (see Blosser, 2017), Christian schools must abandon colorblindness to achieve the unity in diversity of Christ's body. There are biblical rationales for doing so.[1] Colorblindness may be a regulative ideal of how things are in heaven, but that confuses God's Kingdom with ours. Acting colorblind for Christians, then, is to act as if the Kingdom of Heaven already exists on Earth when it does not. And colorblindness is almost always a mechanism for normalizing whiteness, which prevents any true unity from forming among God's diverse creation.

As I see it, unity in diversity as a concept is noble in that it acknowledges the freedom of people to choose to come together in support of a common mission—that of following Christ. But that unity cannot be achieved under conditions in which individual freedoms are stifled and some members of the community are valued less or rendered subservient. Unity cannot be a melting pot. Derek Hicks (2018) says, instead, we need to think of unity as more of a gumbo, where each flavor and texture is distinct yet it makes a beautiful whole. If GA wants unity in the diversity of God's creation, then it needs to intentionally celebrate difference, provide genuine freedom of choice to choose Christ, and create a culture of inclusion, not authoritarianism.

I want to end this book where I began it—with a comment on my social position and what it means. I know that I was allowed access to GA and got the data I did because I was deemed to be enough of a fit. I own that the color of my skin, my religious identity, my gender, and my sexual orientation afforded me the opportunity to conduct research at GA that researchers with other demographics couldn't get. I am also aware that my fit in GA's white institutional space made it easier for me to form relationships with GA stakeholders and harder for me to critique their practices. This is the messy part of ethnographic research for which no textbook or course could have prepared me. But this book wouldn't exist had I not fit at Grace Academy. And I told its story as I experienced it. As Angie Thomas (2017) writes in her poignant novel *The Hate U Give*,

> That's the problem. We let people say stuff, and they say it so much that it becomes okay to them and normal for us. What's the point of having a voice if you're gonna be silent in those moments you shouldn't be?
>
> (p. 252)

Her words get at the very heart of white oppression, of which I've no doubt participated. My hope is that the voices, experiences, policies, and practices described in this book disrupt what's normal in so many predominantly white schools.

In the end, GA's story has something to teach many school communities in the US as they figure out how to educate our increasingly diverse student population. While GA's context may be unique, its normative whiteness and the challenges it faced are not. Pick up almost any ethnographic study of a minority group in schools and one will read of a hegemonic hidden curriculum of diversity that marginalizes and oppresses, as well as instances of microaggressions, overt discrimination, or resistance to "diversity." Thus, I hope Grace Academy's story will prompt educators to examine critically the policies and practices of their own institutions. In so doing, we can build diverse school communities, where students' backgrounds are represented and honored in the curriculum, where marginalized forms of style and communication are welcomed and fit, and where students are encouraged to recognize, question, and speak out against injustice.

Note

1 See Blosser, 2017 for examples.

References

Blosser, A. H. (2017). Considerations for addressing diversity in Christian schools. In D. B. Hiatt-Michael (Ed.), *Family and community engagement in faith-based schools* (pp. 33–55). Charlotte, NC: Information Age Publishing, Inc.

Hicks, D. (2018, September) *The intersection of religion and food*. Lecture given at Emerywood Baptist Church, High Point, NC.

Russo, C. J., Soules, K. E., Newman, A. C., & Douglas, S. L. (2018). Private religious schools. In M. D. Waggoner & N. C. Walker (Eds.), *Oxford handbook of religion and American education* (pp. 169–188). New York, NY: Oxford UP.

Thomas, A. (2017). *The hate u give*. New York, NY: Harper Collins.

Appendix
Methodology[1]

I began my research as a phenomenological case study, which is an appropriate ethnographic method when one wants to understand the particularities of a phenomenon through in-depth study of it (Stake, 1995; Yin, 2009). I set out to examine sensemaking about diversity in a specific context: a conservative Christian school. My goal was to understand the process of sensemaking "from the perspective of the person or persons being studied," a central tenet of phenomenological research (Willis, 2007, p. 107). But consistent with ethnographic research, my research questions evolved as I spent time at GA (Hammersley, 2018).

My research questions were

1. How do stakeholders' (faculty, staff, students, parents, and board members) in a conservative Christian school make sense of diversity?
2. What contextual factors influence school stakeholders' sensemaking about diversity?
3. How do faculty and staff's diversity-related actions and attitudes impact the schooling experiences and learning of students?

Evans (2007) explains that the

> cognitive processes [of sensemaking] manifest themselves through what can be called the 'artifacts' of sensemaking—that is, the words, actions, and behaviors that tell us about the sense that individuals made and may suggest a relationship between meanings made and specific words, actions, and behaviors.
>
> (p. 162)

Therefore, qualitative methods that require attention to words and actions, like interviewing, observation, and document analysis, are logical methods for studying sensemaking. Goldstein (2004) and Coburn (2001) have found the single-case design, in particular, to be well suited to studying organizational sensemaking because the design encourages meticulous examination of sensemaking processes.

I soon discovered that sensemaking about diversity was complex and could not be understood or described without a deep understanding of the shared beliefs and behaviors that defined GA's culture. I knew I needed more time observing everyday life at the school and to conduct more interviews than had I originally intended, so I filed an amendment to my IRB application to interview more participants and adjusted my schedule so that I could spend a full calendar year at GA. My methods then began to reflect those of traditional ethnography in terms of time in the field and "engagement with the data" (Parker-Jenkins, 2018, p. 29). As numerous scholars (e.g., Cohen & Court, 2003; Hammersley, 2018; Parker-Jenkins, 2018) have pointed out, though, the definitions of case study and ethnography are overlapping and blurred.

Further, as I began to understand the patterns of belief and school culture, I also started to recognize the impact of hegemonic and racialized norms and practices on all students, but particularly students of color and other minority students. I realized that sharing my findings and recommendations with the school could be used to bring about change in the school community and had the potential to positively impact marginalized student experiences, so my ethnographic approach became more critical in nature.

Sampling Criteria

GA was an ideal research site for many reasons.[2] As I was deciding where to conduct my study, it was important that the school I selected had some sort of diversity initiative because that meant that the school engaged (presumably) in diversity-related activities, making the school an "information-rich" case to study (Patton, 2002, p. 230). I determined that GA had a diversity initiative in place because one of the goals in the school's 2010–2015 strategic plan was to faithfully integrate diversity into the culture of the school. Likewise, I sought a school that enrolled students from an array of religious backgrounds since religious and/or denominational affiliation has been found to be an important source of diversity in Christian schools.[3] GA boasted that over 350 churches were represented in the school (Blosser, 2017).

The practice of evangelism was also a criterion, because it helped me distinguish a conservative Christian school from a mainline Christian school, which I deemed significant because conservative Christian schools, in particular, have a reputation for having homogeneous student populations and a history of discriminatory practices. Prior research (i.e., Peshkin, 1986; Rose, 1988) also suggests that the cultures of conservative Christian schools are often defined by their religious ideologies, making them good places to study the influence of religious context on sensemaking. In addition, evangelical organizations have a vested interest in instilling cultural competence since evangelism is about sending people into the world to spread a religious message, as opposed to fundamentalism, which typically stresses insularity (Rose, 1988). Two of the strategies in Grace's (2010) strategic plan helped me identify the school as evangelical: 1) the development of a mechanism through which the school can evaluate students' spiritual growth and inclinations toward evangelism and mission work and 2) the creation of opportunities for students to evangelize and participate in mission work. In addition, one of Grace Academy's (2012) desired student outcomes listed on its website was for students to "fulfill the Great Commission," which refers to the resurrected Jesus's charge in Matthew 28 to spread Christianity around the world.

I wanted to study a school that identified itself as college preparatory because many colleges and universities emphasize diversity, global citizenship, and/or cultural competence in their missions and activities (Blosser, 2017), and I suspected that colleges might exert pressure on college-preparatory schools to produce students fit for them, thereby influencing the school's diversity-related activities. GA identified as college preparatory in all of its publications.

Finally, it was important that the school be accredited because I suspected that an accrediting agency could influence the school's diversity-related activities. Further, I knew that accreditation meant that the school would be part of a body of schools that met a set of standards for all schools, which could increase the relevance of my study to other schools. Grace Academy was accredited by two organizations: ACSI and the Southern Association of Colleges and Schools (SACS) (Blosser, 2017).

Participant Recruitment and Informed Consent

I identified participants in multiple ways. I sought participants who represented a range of races, ethnic groups, religious affiliations, income levels, ages, and years involved with the school. But I also sought participants based on their potential to be rich sources of information about the school's construction of diversity, which meant seeking individuals who were particularly interested in or involved in the diversity initiatives of the school. Consistent with sensemaking theory, I considered individuals' roles at the school, their background characteristics, and/or their life experiences as criteria for offering rich information. I also selected participants to recruit based on what I learned from conducting fieldwork at the school or from other participants via snowball sampling in which I asked participants whom else I should interview.

In order to recruit faculty and staff, I introduced myself and described the study at one of the school's monthly staff meetings. I also distributed a handout about the study that included the study's topic, time commitments, and benefits for the school. In my presentation and in the information I distributed, I explained that I was interested in interviewing faculty/staff from a range of racial and ethnic backgrounds, from a variety of religious traditions, and with a range of experience at the school. I explained that I wanted all major subjects represented, as well as staff in a variety of roles. I told faculty and staff that I'd like to interview anyone who conducted any diversity-related activities at the school, including classroom lessons. I explained that in addition to the people mentioned earlier, I'd like to talk with anyone who had a strong interest in or opinion about diversity, or those who felt that their faith strongly shaped their attitudes toward diversity. I thought that these criteria might help me to get "information-rich" participants (Patton, 2002, p. 230). I asked them to contact me if they were interested in participating in the study, and I gained four participants this way. I recruited the remaining faculty/staff participants by reaching out to them, providing them with study information, and asking them to contact me if they would like to participate.

I recruited the one board member I interviewed after he was recommended to me by Dr. Smith. I then reached out to him, offered him study information, and asked him to contact me if he was interested in participating.

Parent and student recruitment followed different procedures. In order to identify potential parent participants, I explained the aforementioned sampling criteria to several of the school's administrators and asked them to identify individuals who met those criteria. There were also a few parents whom I identified as potential participants based on what I learned during the course of the study. The IRB responsible for approving my study did not think it was reasonable for me to ask the school for any family's contact information, so the school contacted potential parent participants and provided them with study information and my contact information should they wish to participate. At that point, parents either contacted me directly or gave the school permission to share their contact information with me.

IRB had much of the same concerns in how I recruited students as it did with the parents. Therefore, the school had to provide students with study information, and then students or parents could contact me with questions about the study. Initially, I explained my sampling criteria to school administrators, and they helped me identify potential participants. After I had been conducting research at the school for a while and learned about many of the students, I was able to identify potential student participants. I asked the school to send home study information to those students. I selected students to ensure I had students representing a wide array of background characteristics and interests. For example, I decided I wanted the perspectives of an exchange student, students who had been on the Dominican Republic mission trip, and black males who did not play football, so the school sent home information to students meeting those criteria upon my request.

In terms of gaining participant consent, IRB recommended that I request a waiver of documentation of informed consent for every participant group except students since the consent form would be the only form linking the participant to the study. In addition, the study presented only minimal risk to participants and involved no procedures for which written consent is generally required outside of the research context. Therefore, I provided all adult participants with a consent form, answered any questions they had, and acquired their verbal consent to participate in the study. All students, regardless of their ages, were required to get a parental consent form signed and sign a student assent form.

Data Collection

I collected data for a full year, beginning in the winter of 2013 and going through the winter of 2014, so across two different school years. Some weeks, I was only at the school one day per week; other weeks, I was there all five days. I conducted student focus groups, interviewed individuals, analyzed school documents, and observed activities.[4]

Observation

I selected the events I observed by their relevance to my study. As Stake (1995) explains, "The plan of observation is directed by the issue" (p. 61). Accordingly, I developed an observation protocol that was responsive to my research questions. My observation protocol and research questions dictated that I observe both special events and daily school activities. Daily school activities allowed me to get a feel for the school culture and recognize patterns in school stakeholders' behaviors, like the fact that female teachers at the school never sat with the male teachers or that African American students tended to sit together at school events. Overall, I observed a wide array of school activities.

I observed daily activities, such as lunch, hallway interactions, dismissal, chapel services, morning meetings, and lunch. I also sat in on classes across subject and grade levels, though I spent the most time in classes that I suspected and/or was told would incorporate diversity, like history, English, foreign language, and Bible/religion. I made sure to observe lessons that weren't covering any special topic related to diversity and those that were. I also accompanied students on five off-campus service projects, such as serving meals at the local homeless shelter, volunteering with Special Olympics, and an event in which students and parents washed the feet of community residents and then provided them with a new pair of shoes. I attended over 20 special events, such as the school's awards ceremony at the end of the year, senior chapel, graduation, Arts Appreciation Day, a Latin[5] festival, sporting events, and Field Day, as well as admissions and guidance office events, such as school tours, open houses, ninth-grade orientation, and new parent orientation. I also observed several faculty/staff meetings. Finally, I paid attention to objects (posters, art, flags, etc.) around the school, because those objects can reflect a school's culture and values. I described those objects in my field notes. My observation protocol guided me as I crafted field notes about the activities I observed. Specifically, it guided me to pay attention to not only the activity itself but also the physical and social settings of the activities, as well as the tone and nature of interactions between various stakeholders.

I took extensive field notes on my observations of school activities. While observing, my role was largely "observer as participant," which means I "observe[d] and interact[ed] closely enough with members to establish an insider's identity without participating in those activities constituting the core of group membership" (Adler & Adler, 1998, as cited in Merriam, 2009, p. 124). There were a few times, however, in which a participant put me on the spot and asked me to help him/her with a task or to contribute to a conversation. For example, a teacher once left her classroom in the middle of teaching, and she asked me to help lead class discussion. Another time, I was following along on an admissions tour, and I was asked to explain my study to a parent who was concerned about her daughter, an ethnic minority student, fitting in. But as I mention in the book's introduction, I believe I achieved insider status because the administration trusted me with the school's keys and security code, and I was invited to sit with staff at graduation. In addition, participants eventually began ignoring my presence so that I was able to observe "real life" at the school.

Documents

Documents were important to my study because it was through them that GA projected an image of itself. Documents also provided evidence of school policies, practices, and values. In selecting documents for analysis, I looked for indications of the school's identity, mission, and goals, for any mention of diversity, for indications of the religious beliefs of the school, and for indications of contextual influences upon the school. Thus, I collected documents such as "GA's website, strategic plan, student handbook, accreditation reports, job contracts, demographic reports," etc. (Blosser, 2017, p. 40). I also collected curricular artifacts (lesson plans, assignments, readings, etc.) in which difference was discussed or diverse viewpoints presented (Blosser, 2017).

Individual Interviews

I conducted semi-structured individual interviews with an array of stakeholders within the school (board members, faculty and staff, parents, and students) so that I could compare their perspectives. The semi-structured nature of the interviews allowed me to seek specific information from individuals, but it also allowed subsequent questions to emerge naturally from the conversation. The flexibility of semi-structured interviews was particularly important to my study since I was researching the highly personal process of sensemaking about a sensitive topic, and I was able to ask clarifying questions when needed. As Merriam (2009) says of semi-structured interviews, "This format allows the researcher to respond to the situation at hand, to the emerging worldview of the respondent, and to new ideas on the topic" (p. 90). Using my conceptual framework, I developed interview protocols for each stakeholder group that included open-ended questions, as well as basic demographic questions. I made sure to ask participants about prior experiences, personal religious beliefs, and personal attitudes about diversity, as sensemaking theory maintains that such attitudes and experiences shape sensemaking.

I conducted individual interviews with 60 people. Most interviews averaged about an hour, though interviews with administrators tended to last closer to two hours, and I conducted follow-up interviews with some participants. All interviews were audio recorded and later transcribed. I also had countless conversations with participants in the hallways and at events, which were documented via field notes.

GA employed 116 total faculty and staff. I interviewed 12 staff members, which included administrators; support staff, such as secretaries and cafeteria workers; admissions and development staff; guidance and college counselors; and coaches. I interviewed 14 teachers. When selecting teachers, I made sure to recruit teachers from all levels (elementary, middle, high) to get a full view of sensemaking about diversity at the school and to be able to draw comparisons across divisions. I also made sure to have all of the major subjects represented, as well as physical education, fine arts, foreign language, and religion. When students repeatedly claimed that they learned about diversity in a specific course, I sought out the teacher of that course to participate in the study. I interviewed 3 teachers who had been at the school less than 5 years, 7 teachers who had been at the school between 5 and 15 years, and 4 teachers who had been at the school over 15 years.

I interviewed 13 parents, not including faculty and staff members who also identified as parents of Grace Academy students.[6] I interviewed parents of children across all divisions. I made sure to interview relatively new parents to the school and parents whose children had been attending the school for a long time. I made sure to interview a parent on the board of the PTO. I also made sure to interview parents from a range of different ethnic backgrounds and parents who had children of various ethnicities.[7] I also interviewed a grandparent who was the legal guardian of two students. The school had strict policies in terms of who had access to and/or knowledge of parents' financial situations, so I was not able to intentionally recruit parent participants according to their socioeconomic status. A few of the parent participants wished to be interviewed with their spouses, and one parent was the spouse of a school employee.

I interviewed 20 students from various grades in the high school.[8] I interviewed students from a range of racial and ethnic backgrounds, as well as lengths of time attending the school. I also made sure to interview students with a range of religious affiliations, including Catholic (a rarity at the school). I interviewed a foreign exchange student. Like with the parents, the school's policies prevented me from intentionally recruiting student participants according to their socioeconomic statuses.

Finally, I interviewed one board member. I did not choose to interview any other board members because I learned early on from interview data and field notes that the board had little to do with the creation or implementation of diversity activities at the school, and thus board members would not generally be rich sources of information.

Focus Groups

I conducted two focus groups with 11 (total) students at the school. As Macnaghten and Myers claim, "Focus groups work best for topics people could talk about to each other in their everyday lives—but don't" (as cited in Merriam, 2009, p. 94). I reasoned that focus groups were appropriate because diversity is a weighty and abstract issue to tackle, and diversity, especially as it relates to race, is not often discussed explicitly in schools (Pollock, 2004). I thought that students might feel more comfortable discussing diversity in groups. That said, I also recognized that for some people, diversity could be a sensitive issue and that being part of a group discussion could preclude them from sharing their honest thoughts and feelings, especially given that my focus groups included students from different racial backgrounds. This is why I followed up focus groups with individual interviews.[9] My focus group questions were designed to encourage group dialogue about diversity at Grace Academy. They were primarily questions about the school's courses and practices, as opposed to individual experiences, beliefs, and attitudes. Those questions I saved for individual interviews with students. In my follow-up interviews with students, I also asked some students to elaborate on things they said in the focus group or on assertions made in their group.

Data Analysis

I collected data until I achieved saturation—that is, until I was seeing and hearing the same things over and over again (Merriam, 2009). Consistent with qualitative research, I analyzed data as I was collecting it and after it was complete (Blosser, 2017). As I reviewed interview transcripts, field notes, and school documents, I regularly wrote analytic memos about my findings. I used the analytic memos to determine themes, which later became codes for analyzing my data.

For my first round of coding,

> I utilized a combination of *descriptive coding*, in which I developed codes from my data and analytic memos, *provisional coding*, in which I developed codes from my conceptual framework, and *structural coding*, in which I developed codes from my research questions.
>
> (Saldana, 2013; Blosser, 2017, p. 40)

After I developed a code list from these methods, I exhaustively coded my data using NVivo coding software. Consistent with first-round coding techniques, my initial code list was quite long (Saldana, 2013).

I began my second round of coding by reviewing the material I had assigned to each code and creating matrix displays of the relationships between various codes. From these matrices, I crafted analytic memos exploring the relationships in more depth. These matrices and memos helped me to recognize patterns in the codes I had developed (Miles, Huberman, & Saldana, 2014). The overarching patterns I identified became the primary codes, while the prior long list of codes became subcodes. I also ensured that my codes were "sensitive to the data," "responsive to the purpose of the research," and "exhaustive" (Merriam, 2009, pp. 185–186). Finally, my second round of analysis also included "direct interpretation," wherein I analyzed (via writing memos) the meaning of particular instances that I had recorded in my field notes (Stake, 1995, p. 74).

Validity

To ensure the validity of the study, I triangulated sources of data by comparing information gathered from interviews and focus groups to field notes and documents to determine if what the school professed on paper reflected what I observed and heard in interviews (Blosser, 2017). Triangulating data sources is important for "see[ing] if the phenomenon or case remains the same at other times, in other spaces, or as persons interact differently" (Stake, 1995, p. 112). I also utilized member checks (Merriam, 2009) through regularly sharing my analyses with program participants to ensure that my analysis was accurate and to help me determine if there was any contradictory evidence to my interpretations (Blosser, 2017). For example, I noticed early on in data collection that faculty and staff often used the rhetoric of colorblindness when describing their philosophies of education, so I began asking participants specifically about colorblindness to confirm and refine my understanding of its pervasiveness at GA.

Similarly, Katz (1987) claims that to ensure the validity of a phenomenological study, the researcher must become aware of her own biases concerning the phenomenon so that she can "see the experience for itself" (as cited in Merriam, 2009, p. 199). There were several practices I engaged in to become aware of my biases. Foremost, I practiced reflexivity through regularly writing memos in which I was able to "bracket" my personal opinions and distinguish them from the recorded data (Merriam, 2009, p. 25). Moreover, I also practiced "phenomenological reduction," "horizontalization," and "imaginative variation" throughout the analysis process (Merriam, 2009, p. 26). Practicing phenomenological reduction meant that I focused my attention on the actual phenomenon (as opposed to my opinion) as it surfaced in the data so that I could capture the phenomenon's essence. Practicing horizontalization meant that during analysis, I gave each piece of data equal weight so to control for my biases. Finally, imaginative variation required me to view the phenomenon through the lenses of each of the school's stakeholder and minority groups so to present a full picture of the phenomenon instead of a one-sided picture. This practice also helped me realize the value of acknowledging students as sensemakers within schools.

Limitations

The biggest limitation of my study was that I only studied a single site, which limits the generalizability of my results (Merriam, 2009; Stake, 1995). Generalizability, however, was not the main goal of my research. As Stake (1995) argues, the real purpose for case study and ethnographic research is "particularization, not generalization" wherein the primary focus is "on understanding the case itself" (p. 8). I chose to study a single site so that I could explore the contextual and phenomenological nuances of organizational sensemaking about diversity in great depth. And, as previously mentioned, my decision to do so was largely based on the reasoning of scholars (e.g., Coburn, 2001; Goldstein, 2004) who found the single-case design to be ideal for studying organizational sensemaking.

Notes

1 See Blosser, 2017 for an abbreviated description of the methodology.
2 See Blosser, 2017 for an abbreviated, bulleted list of sampling criteria.
3 As suggested by Green (2006); Schweber and Irwin (2003), and Wagner (1990, 1997).
4 I also describe my methods of data collection in Blosser, 2017.
5 The language, not the culture.
6 All but four of the faculty and staff participants (so 22) had children who either currently attended or had previously attended the school, so they also identified as parents.

7 I distinguish parents' ethnicities from their children because in two cases, the parent's ethnicity differed from that of their child(ren) due to adoption.
8 The high school consisted of grades 9–12.
9 After I conducted individual interviews with the 11 focus group participants, I identified 9 more students I wanted to interview based on conversations with students, observations of school activities, and my continual assessment of the background characteristics of students represented in my study. I conducted only individual interviews with those nine students.

References

Blosser, A. H. (2017). Considerations for addressing diversity in Christian schools. In D. B. Hiatt-Michael (Ed.), *Family and community engagement in faith-based schools* (pp. 33–55). Charlotte, NC: Information Age Publishing, Inc.

Coburn, C. E. (2001). Collective sensemaking about reading: How teachers mediate reading policy in their professional communities. *Educational Evaluation and Policy Analysis, 23*(2), 145–170.

Cohen, A., & Court, D. (2003). Ethnography and case study: A comparative analysis. *Academic Exchange, 7*(3), 283–287.

Evans, A. E. (2007). School leaders and their sensemaking about race and demographic change. *Educational Administration Quarterly, 43*(2), 159–188.

Goldstein, J. (2004). Making sense of distributed leadership: The case of peer assistance and review. *Educational Evaluation and Policy Analysis, 26*(2), 173–197.

Green, J. (2006). Christ-centered, diverse, and academically excellent. *American Educational History Journal, 33*(1), 89–95.

Hammersley, M. (2018). What is ethnography? Can it survive? Should it? *Ethnography and Education, 13*(1), 1–17.

Katz, L. (1987). *The experience of personal change*. Unpublished doctoral dissertation. Cincinnati, OH: Graduate School, Union Institute.

Macnaghten, P., & Myers, G. (2004). Focus groups. In C. Seale, G. Gobo, J. F. Gubrium, & D. Sliverman (Eds.), *Qualitative research practice* (pp. 65–79). Thousand Oaks, CA: Sage.

Merriam, S. B. (2009). *Qualitative research: A guide to design and implementation*. San Francisco, CA: Jossey-Bass.

Miles, M. B., Huberman, A. H., & Saldana, J. (2014). *Qualitative data analysis* (3rd ed.). Thousand Oaks, CA: Sage Publications, Inc.

Parker-Jenkins, M. (2018). Problematising ethnography and case study: Reflections on using ethnographic techniques and researcher positioning. *Ethnography and Education, 13*(1), 18–33.

Patton, M. Q. (2002). *Qualitative research and evaluation methods* (3rd ed.). Thousand Oaks, CA: Sage.

Peshkin, A. (1986). *God's choice: The total world of a fundamentalist Christian school*. Chicago, IL: University of Chicago Press.

Pollock, M. (2004). *Colormute: Race talk dilemmas in an American school*. Princeton, NJ: Princeton UP.

Rose, S. (1988). *Keeping them out of the hands of Satan: Evangelical schooling in America*. New York, NY: Routledge, Chapman and Hall, Inc.

Saldana, J. (2013). *The coding manual for qualitative researchers*. Los Angeles, CA: Sage Publications, Ltd.

Schweber, S., & Irwin, R. (2003). "Especially special": Learning about Jews in a fundamentalist Christian school. *Teachers College Record, 105*(9), 1693–1719.

Stake, R. E. (1995). *The art of case-study research*. Thousand Oaks, CA: Sage.

Wagner, M. B. (1990). *God's schools: Choice and compromise in American society*. New Brunswick, NJ: Rutgers University Press.

Wagner, M. B. (1997). Generic conservative Christianity: The demise of denominationalism in Christian schools. *Journal for the Scientific Study of Religion, 36*(1), 13–24.

Willis, J. W. (2007). *Foundations of qualitative research: Interpretive and critical approaches*. Thousand Oaks, CA: Sage Publications, Inc.

Yin, R. K. (2009). *Case study research: Design and methods* (4th ed.). Thousand Oaks, CA: Sage.

Note: I exclude references that might in any way compromise the identity of the school.

Index

ability 32, 93–94
accreditation 10–11, 13, 29–30, 37, 42n7, 127–128, 142, 145
admission: admissions staff 26, 87n7, 146; at Christian schools 2, 8–9, 50; at GA 9–10, 26, 35–36, 41, 46–51, 64, 74, 99–100, 123, 125, 127, 130, 144–145; GA's application for admission 9–10, 48, 65n6; at Lighthouse Christian Academy 1; at Myrtle Grove Christian School 8; Obama-era admissions guidelines 122; in white organizations 63, 82
Affirmative Action 35, 52, 122
AP Biology 107, 110, 119
Association of Christian Schools International (ASCI) as accrediting organization 18n1, 29, 42n7, 130, 142; recommendations of 13, 29–30, 37, 40–41; researcher support from 13–14
athlete *see* athletics
athletics 16, 26, 48, 70–78, 85–86, 87n7n9, 92, 121, 127
authority 11, 26–28, 40, 57, 109–110, 137

Bible 3, 14–15, 18n1, 26–27, 32, 49, 106, 108–111, *114*, 115n9; Bible classes 56, 101, 105, 108, 144; biblical approach to diversity 15, 31–32, 36, 38, 42, 49–50, 69, 84, 86, 136–137; biblical curriculum 7, 92; biblical references 31, 32–33, 58, 65n11, 69, 87, 106, 123; biblical worldview/perspective 7, 26, 69, 84, 86, 130; Policy on Biblical Living 92, 99–104, 113–114, 119

Bob Jones University v. United States 2
Brown vs. Board of Education 2

Catholic: Catholicism 109; people 107, 109, 147; schools 26
case study 122, 140–141, 149
Choices in Education Act 5
Christian School Movement 3
Christian Unity and Diversity Coordinator *see* diversity coordinator
colorblindness: author's perception of 137; in cultivating school climate 79, 82–86; in recruiting/retaining students and teachers of color 45–46, 49–58, 62–64, 118; school changes concerning colorblindness 126, 131; in sensemaking about GA's diversity initiative 33–37, 41, 118, 122
community service *see* service opportunities
Critical Race Theory (CRT) 43, 45, 50, 68, 85, 99
culturally relevant pedagogy (CRP) 57–58, 83–86, 87n13, 90, 92, 119–122, 131–132
curated diversity 120–121

democracy 8, 19n8, 110; democratic citizenship 7–8; Democratic Party 60; democratic society 2, 7, 112
Devos, B. 1, 5
disability *see* ability
discrimination: in Christian schools 1–2, 8–9, 123, 137, 141; at GA 18, 50, 99, 131; at other schools 73, 138; reverse discrimination 79
diversity coordinator 46, 55, 68–72, 74–75, 78, 85–86, 92, 131

Index

diversity initiative: buy in of 39–41, 122, 132–133; components of 31–32, 45, 50, 53, 64, 68–69, 75, 113, 118; creation of 13, 29–33; faculty and staff attitudes about 33–38, 74–75, 91; as sampling criteria 141–142

diversity statement: development of 30–32, 35, 38–40, 133; in the enrollment agreement 129; implementation of 45, 68, 74–75, 84, 90, 105, 113, 119

employment *see* hiring practices

ethnicity 30, 32, 42, 45–46, 50, 62, 69, 78, 86, 99; ethnic breakdown of student population 125, 128, 133; ethnic diversity of Cedar Ridge 25; ethnic diversity in service opportunities 93–94; ethnic diversity of the U.S. 5, 30; ethnicity in the curriculum 105; ethnicity of participants 142, 146–147, 150n7; interethnic friendships 8; stereotyping/jokes about ethnicity 40, 80

ethnography 10, 17, 110, 123, 138, 140–141, 149

evangelical: black evangelicals 60; evangelical Christianity 107; evangelicalism 3, 120; evangelical mission/values 36, 38; evangelical organizations 15, 25, 75, 130, 141–142; evangelicals (general) 1, 3–5, 13, 19, 34, 96, 103, 105, 137; white evangelicals 3, 5, 34, 37, 53–54, 60, 63–64, 79, 95, 120–122

evangelism 31, 38, *114*, 141–142

femininity *see* gender, gender norms

fit: of researcher 138; of students 45–50, 62, 64, 82, 118, 123, 127, 129–130, 138; of teachers 45, 50–58, 61–64, 118, 121, 131–132

football 46–47, 70–78, 81, 85, 87n6n7n9, 92, 95, 119, 143

Fourth Great Awakening 3

gender: beliefs about women's role 2, 56; in the curriculum 91, 93; gendered experiences of black students 75–79, 81, 86; gender identity 1, 137; gender norms 45, 55–57, 62, 92, 144; policies concerning gender 1, 99, 115n9, 129–130; researcher gender 138; secular conceptions of 31; transgender 1, 8

hidden curriculum 90–93, 99, 103–104, 113–114, 122, 138

hiring practices: conditions for employment 8, 25, 27, 35–36, 41, 51, 54, 65n11, 115n9, 125; hiring a diversity coordinator 46, 55, 68–75, 78, 85; hiring and targets/quotas 35–36, 119; hiring teachers of color 46, 50–52, 55, 61–63, 125, 132; qualifications of hires 35, 51, 55, 61–62, 64

heterosexuality *see* sexual orientation

homosexuality *see* sexual orientation

House of Representatives Bill 610 *see* Choices in Education Act

identity: organizational identity 11, 39, 42, 59, 64, 74–75, 118, 121, 137, 145; personal identity 12, 31–32, 81, 91, 93, 95, 100, 103–105, 109, 111–113, 119–120, 122, 130, 137; researcher identity 13–18, 125, 136, 138, 145

ideology: Christian ideology 26, 31, 34, 41, 42n12, 45, 50, 103, 122; colorblind ideology 50, 58; definition of 42; ideological contradictions 53; ideological health 124; ideological opposition 4; organizational ideology 12, 26–27, 30–31, 41, 52, 58, 62, 92, 103, 110, 118, 122–123, 136, 141

insider-outsider *see* identity, researcher identity

integration 2, 26, 30, 47, 69, 76, 123, 128, 141

Islam 104, 106, 108, 110, 115n10

King, M. L. Jr. 34, 42n10n11, 55, 60, 131

legitimizing myth 52–53, 62

LGBTQ *see* sexual orientation

mainline Christian *see* mainline Protestant

mainline Protestant 4, 13, 20, 24, 26, 107, 109, 141

Index

mission: mission trip 16, 94, 96–98, 143; mission work 31, 90, 93, 97, 142; school mission 12–13, 26, 30, 38, 47, 92, 112–113, 123, 127, 129, 133, 142, 145
multicultural instruction 37, 58, 91, 104
multiculturalism 31

Obama, B. 55–56, 59–60, 122
open system 11, 38
organizational theory 10, 21
outsider *see* identity, researcher identity

political norms 35, 45, 55–60, 62, 79, 127
Postmodernism 31, 104, 107

racism: antiracist work 136; concerning GA 18, 37, 40, 52, 54, 84, *114*; in schools 75, 84, 110; in white communities 39, 54, 79, 95, 120

sampling criteria 13, 19, 141–143
secular: secular aid 6; secular culture 9, 14, 15, 17, 27, 30–31, 36, 38–39, 107, *114*, 119, 123, 130, 136; secular curriculum 104; secular humanism 4, 19; secularism 31, 118; secular nature of public schools 4; secularization of churches 4; secular perspectives 9, 14, 17, 31, 103–104, 107, 118–119, 123, 131, 133; secular private schools 26, 30, 69, 101, 113
segregation 2, 25, 64, 111, 123
sensemaking : of administrators 30–32, 38–39, 45–47, 50–53, 62, 64, 74, 119; characteristics of 10–13, 29, 53, 74, 91–92, 99–100, 119, 140–142, 146, 149; of faculty and staff 33, 36, 103, 119, 122; of stakeholders 52, 75, 91–92, 118, 140; of students 92, 95, 99–100, 103, 108, 11
service learning *see* service opportunities
service opportunities 10, 73, 90, 92–99, 104, 113–114, 115n6n7n8, 144
sexual orientation: and Christian schools 2, 8–9, 124, 129, 137; in the curriculum 99–103, 108, 113–114; as defined in GA's diversity statement/initiative 32, 36, 113, 119; in enrollment or employment policies 1, 8, 27, 99–103, *114*, 115n9, 129–130; evangelical stances on 103, 137; identity and beliefs of the researcher 13, 136, 138; in service opportunities 115n3
social class *see* socioeconomic status
social position *see* identity, researcher identity
socioeconomic status: attitudes attributed to race/class 54, 121; in the diversity initiative 32, 36, 42, 45; in the hidden curriculum 91, 93–94, 99; of participants 146–147; of students 5, 74, 76–77, 127–128
stereotype 40, 72–79, 84–87, 95–96, 121

theology: of black churches 74; of Christians 34, 84, 119; of Christian schools 7, 11, 18n1n2, 123–124, 136–137; of GA 16, 26, 31–33, 42n6, 58, 60, 103, 110, 118; of the researcher 14–16; of Understanding the Times 104–105
transgender *see* gender
Trinity Lutheran Church of Columbia, Inc. V. Comer 6
Trump, D. 1, 3, 5, 122

Understanding the Times (UTT) 104–108, 111, 119
unity: Christian unity 49, 53, 57–58, 62, 69, 74, 121; disunity 120; unity in Christ 32, 34, 41, 45, 49–50, 53, 63–64, 99, 120; unity in diversity 31–33, 42n11, 75, 84–86, 98–99, 137

validity 148–149
vouchers 1–2, 5–10, 19n7, 56, 112, 118, 120–121, 123, 126–128, 134n1

white flight 26, 71
white fragility 21, 120–121
worldview 7, 12–13, 17, 27–28, 30, 103–*114*, 146

Zelman v. Simmons-Harris 6